THE TEMPEST

DOVER THRIFT EDITIONS

William Shakespeare

DOVER PUBLICATIONS, INC.
GARDEN CITY, NEW YORK

DOVER THRIFT EDITIONS

GENERAL EDITOR: PAUL NEGRI
EDITOR OF THIS VOLUME: RONALD HERDER

Theatrical Rights

This Dover Thrift Edition may be used in its entirety, in adaptation, or in any other way for theatrical productions, professional and amateur, in the United States, without fee, permission, or acknowledgment. (This may not apply outside of the United States, as copyright conditions may vary.)

Bibliographical Note

This Dover edition, first published in 1999, contains the unabridged text of *The Tempest* as published in Volume VIII of *The Caxton Edition of the Complete Works of William Shakespeare*, Caxton Publishing Company, London, n.d. The Note was prepared specially for this edition.

Library of Congress Cataloging-in-Publication Data

Shakespeare, William, 1564–1616.
    The tempest / William Shakespeare.
        p.   cm. — (Dover thrift editions)
    ISBN-13: 978-0-486-40658-9 (pbk.)
    ISBN-10: 0-486-40658-X (pbk.)
    1. Survival after shipwrecks, etc—Drama. 2. Fathers and daughters—Drama. 3. Castaways—Drama. 4. Magicians—Drama. I. Title. II. Series.
[PR2833.A1   1999]
822.3'3—dc21   99-11771
                                                                CIP

Manufactured in the United States by LSC Communications
40658X16   2020
www.doverpublications.com

Note

The Tempest is Shakespeare's last play and as such occupies a special place in the canon of his works. While some have suggested that the first performance was in February of 1613 in celebration of the marriage of Princess Elizabeth and Frederick V, the first performance was more likely at court in 1611. A story of adventure and misadventure on an enchanted island, the play is populated by some of Shakespeare's most memorable characters: Prospero, philosopher and magician; his innocent, unworldly daughter Miranda; his treacherous brother Alonso; the handsome Prince Ferdinand; the magical sprite Ariel; and the beastly Caliban.

Scholars and critics have seen the play as an allegory on man's relationship to nature, an exploration of life's blending of reality and illusion, Shakespeare's final meditations on art and philosophy, and have offered myriad other thematic analyses. The play's richness and complexity support these and other interpretations. What is beyond debate is the play's profundity of thought and extraordinary beauty of language, qualities that have made it a favorite with scholars and audiences alike. Henry James said of *The Tempest*, "It affects us, taking its complexity and perfection together, as the rarest of all examples of literary art."

Contents

Dramatis Personæ[1]

ALONSO, King of Naples.
SEBASTIAN, his brother.
PROSPERO, the right Duke of Milan.
ANTONIO, his brother, the usurping Duke of Milan.
FERDINAND, son to the King of Naples.
GONZALO, an honest old Counsellor.
ADRIAN,
FRANCISCO, } Lords.
CALIBAN, a savage and deformed Slave.
TRINCULO, a Jester.
STEPHANO, a drunken Butler.
Master of a Ship.
Boatswain
Mariners.

MIRANDA, daughter to Prospero.

ARIEL, an airy Spirit.
IRIS,
CERES,
JUNO, } presented by Spirits.
Nymphs,
Reapers,

Other Spirits attending on Prospero.

SCENE—*A ship at sea: an uninhabited island.*

---

[1]*The Tempest* was first published in the First Folio of 1623, and is the opening play of that volume. It is there divided into Acts and Scenes, and the stage directions are exceptionally full. At the close of the piece "The Scene" is described as "an uninhabited island," and a list of the dramatis personæ is given under the heading "Names of the Actors."

ACT I.

On a ship at sea: a tempestuous noise
of thunder and lightning heard.

Enter A SHIP-MASTER *and* A BOATSWAIN.

MAST.   Boatswain!

BOATS.   Here, master: what cheer?

MAST.   Good, speak to the mariners: fall to 't, yarely,[1] or we run our-
selves aground: bestir, bestir.   [*Exit.*

Enter MARINERS.

BOATS.   Heigh, my hearts! cheerly, cheerly, my hearts! yare, yare!
Take in the topsail. Tend to the master's whistle. Blow, till thou
burst thy wind, if room enough![2]

Enter ALONSO, SEBASTIAN, ANTONIO, FERDINAND, GONZALO, *and*
others.

ALON.   Good boatswain, have care. Where's the master? Play the
men.

BOATS.   I pray now, keep below.

ANT.   Where is the master, boatswain?

BOATS.   Do you not hear him? You mar our labour: keep your cabins:
you do assist the storm.

GON.   Nay, good,[3] be patient.

BOATS.   When the sea is. Hence! What cares these roarers for the
name of king? To cabin: silence! trouble us not.

GON.   Good, yet remember whom thou hast aboard.

BOATS.   None that I more love than myself. You are a counsellor; if
you can command these elements to silence, and work the peace

---

[1]*yarely*] briskly, readily.
[2]*Blow . . . room enough*] The boatswain addresses the storm. His anxiety is about the sea
room at his disposal rather than about the force of the gale.
[3]*good*] my good fellow.

1

of the present, we will not hand a rope more; use your authority: if you cannot, give thanks you have lived so long, and make yourself ready in your cabin for the mischance of the hour, if it so hap. Cheerly, good hearts! Out of our way, I say.   [*Exit.*

GON. I have great comfort from this fellow: methinks he hath no drowning mark upon him; his complexion is perfect gallows. Stand fast, good Fate, to his hanging: make the rope of his destiny our cable, for our own doth little advantage. If he be not born to be hanged, our case is miserable.   [*Exeunt.*

Re-enter BOATSWAIN.

BOATS. Down with the topmast! yare! lower, lower! Bring her to try with main-course.[4] [*A cry within.*] A plague upon this howling! they are louder than the weather or our office.

Re-enter SEBASTIAN, ANTONIO, *and* GONZALO.

Yet again! what do you here? Shall we give o'er, and drown? Have you a mind to sink?

SEB. A pox o' your throat, you bawling, blasphemous, incharitable dog!

BOATS. Work you, then.

ANT. Hang, cur! hang, you whoreson, insolent noise-maker. We are less afraid to be drowned than thou art.

GON. I 'll warrant him for drowning;[5] though the ship were no stronger than a nutshell, and as leaky as an unstanched wench.

BOATS. Lay her a-hold, a-hold! set her two courses;[6] off to sea again; lay her off.

Enter MARINERS *wet.*

MARINERS. All lost! to prayers, to prayers! all lost!

BOATS. What, must our mouths be cold?[7]

GON. The king and prince at prayers! let 's assist them,
     For our case is as theirs.

SEB.   I 'm out of patience.

ANT. We are merely cheated of our lives by drunkards:
     This wide-chapp'd rascal,—would thou mightst lie drowning
     The washing of ten tides![8]

[4]*main-course*] mainsail.
[5]*for drowning*] against drowning.
[6]*set her two courses*] set the foresail as well as the mainsail.
[7]*must our mouths be cold?*] must we die?
[8]*washing of ten tides*] a grotesque reference to the punishment allotted at the time to pirates and sea robbers, to be hanged at low water, and to be left till *three* tides had washed over them.

GON.   He 'll be hang'd yet,
    Though every drop of water swear against it,
    And gape at widest to glut[9] him.
    [*A confused noise within*: "Mercy on us!" —
    "We split, we split!" — "Farewell my wife and children!" —
    "Farewell, brother!" — "We split, we split, we split!"]
ANT.   Let 's all sink with the king.
SEB.   Let 's take leave of him.   [*Exeunt Ant. and Seb.*
GON.   Now would I give a thousand furlongs of sea for an acre of bar-
    ren ground, long heath, brown furze, any thing. The wills above
    be done! but I would fain die a dry death.   [*Exeunt.*

SCENE II. *The Island.*

Before PROSPERO's *Cell.*

Enter PROSPERO *and* MIRANDA.

MIR.   If by your art, my dearest father, you have
    Put the wild waters in this roar, allay them.
    The sky, it seems, would pour down stinking pitch,
    But that the sea, mounting to the welkin's cheek,
    Dashes the fire out. O, I have suffer'd
    With those that I saw suffer! a brave vessel,
    Who had, no doubt, some noble creature in her,
    Dash'd all to pieces. O, the cry did knock
    Against my very heart! Poor souls, they perish'd!
    Had I been any god of power, I would
    Have sunk the sea within the earth, or ere
    It should the good ship so have swallow'd and
    The fraughting souls within her.
PROS.   Be collected:
    No more amazement: tell your piteous heart
    There 's no harm done.
MIR.   O, woe the day!
PROS.   No harm.
    I have done nothing but in care of thee,
    Of thee, my dear one, thee, my daughter, who
    Art ignorant of what thou art, nought knowing
    Of whence I am, nor that I am more better

[9]*glut*] swallow.

Than Prospero, master of a full poor cell,
And thy no greater father.
MIR.   More to know
Did never meddle with my thoughts.
PROS.   'T is time
I should inform thee farther. Lend thy hand,
And pluck my magic garment from me. — So:

                                      [Lays down his mantle.

Lie there, my art. Wipe thou thine eyes; have comfort.
The direful spectacle of the wreck, which touch'd
The very virtue of compassion in thee,
I have with such provision in mine art
So safely order'd, that there is no soul,
No, not so much perdition as an hair
Betid to any creature in the vessel
Which thou heard'st cry, which thou saw'st sink. Sit down;
For thou must now know farther.
MIR.   You have often
Begun to tell me what I am; but stopp'd,
And left me to a bootless inquisition,
Concluding "Stay: not yet."
PROS.   The hour 's now come;
The very minute bids thee ope thine ear;
Obey, and be attentive. Canst thou remember
A time before we came unto this cell?
I do not think thou canst, for then thou wast not
Out three years old.[1]
MIR.   Certainly, sir, I can.
PROS.   By what? by any other house or person?
Of any thing the image tell me, that
Hath kept with thy remembrance.
MIR.   'T is far off,
And rather like a dream than an assurance
That my remembrance warrants. Had I not
Four or five women once that tended me?
PROS.   Thou hadst, and more, Miranda. But how is it
That this lives in thy mind? What seest thou else
In the dark backward and abysm[2] of time?
If thou remember'st aught ere thou camest here,
How thou camest here thou mayst.
MIR.   But that I do not.

---

[1]*Out three years*] Full three years.
[2]*backward and abysm*] past and abyss.

PROS.   Twelve year since, Miranda, twelve year since,
            Thy father was the Duke of Milan, and
            A prince of power.

MIR.   Sir, are not you my father?

PROS.   Thy mother was a piece of virtue, and
            She said thou wast my daughter; and thy father
            Was Duke of Milan; and his only heir
            A princess, no worse issued.

MIR.   O the heavens!
            What foul play had we, that we came from thence?
            Or blessed was 't we did?

PROS.   Both, both, my girl:
            By foul play, as thou say'st, were we heaved thence;
            But blessedly holp hither.

MIR.   O, my heart bleeds
            To think o' the teen that I have turn'd you to,
            Which is from my remembrance! Please you, farther.

PROS.   My brother, and thy uncle, call'd Antonio, —
            I pray thee, mark me, — that a brother should
            Be so perfidious! — he whom, next thyself,
            Of all the world I loved, and to him put
            The manage of my state; as at that time
            Through all the signories[3] it was the first,
            And Prospero the prime duke,[4] being so reputed
            In dignity, and for the liberal arts
            Without a parallel; those being all my study,
            The government I cast upon my brother,
            And to my state grew stranger, being transported
            And rapt in secret studies. Thy false uncle —
            Dost thou attend me?

MIR.   Sir, most heedfully.

PROS.   Being once perfected how to grant suits,
            How to deny them, who to advance, and who
            To trash for over-topping,[5] new created
            The creatures that were mine, I say, or changed 'em,
            Or else new form'd 'em; having both the key
            Of officer and office, set all hearts i' the state
            To what tune pleased his ear; that now he was

---

[3] *the signories*] the dukedoms or principalities of Northern Italy.

[4] *the prime duke*] holding the leading place among dukes.

[5] *To trash for over-topping*] To restrain those who were inclined to be too assertive or forward. "To trash" was a hunting term for checking the pace of a hound; "over-topping" is a gardening term for a too luxuriant growth.

The ivy which had hid my princely trunk,
And suck'd my verdure out on 't. Thou attend'st not.
MIR.   O, good sir, I do.
PROS.   I pray thee, mark me.
I, thus neglecting worldly ends, all dedicated
To closeness[6] and the bettering of my mind
With that which, but by being so retired,
O'er-prized all popular rate, in my false brother
Awaked an evil nature; and my trust,
Like a good parent, did beget of him
A falsehood in its contrary, as great
As my trust was; which had indeed no limit,
A confidence sans[7] bound. He being thus lorded,
Not only with what my revenue yielded,
But what my power might else exact, like one
Who having into truth, by telling of it,
Made such a sinner of his memory,
To credit his own lie, he did believe
He was indeed the duke; out o' the substitution,
And executing the outward face of royalty,
With all prerogative:—hence his ambition growing,—
Dost thou hear?
MIR.   Your tale, sir, would cure deafness.
PROS.   To have no screen between this part he play'd
And him he play'd it for, he needs will be
Absolute Milan.[8] Me, poor man, my library
Was dukedom large enough: of temporal royalties
He thinks me now incapable; confederates,
So dry[9] he was for sway, wi' the King of Naples
To give him annual tribute, do him homage,
Subject his coronet to his crown, and bend
The dukedom, yet unbow'd,—alas, poor Milan!—
To most ignoble stooping.
MIR.   O the heavens!
PROS.   Mark his condition, and the event; then tell me
If this might be a brother.
MIR.   I should sin

---

[6]*closeness*] seclusion.
[7]*sans*] the French preposition for "without."
[8]*To have . . . Milan*] To remove everything that lay between the mere role of Duke and
the Duke's own being, between the shadow and the substance of the Duke's authority,
he must needs be actual Duke, Duke without restriction.
[9]*dry*] thirsty, eager.

To think but nobly of my grandmother:
Good wombs have borne bad sons.
PROS.   Now the condition.
This King of Naples, being an enemy
To me inveterate, hearkens my brother's suit;
Which was, that he, in lieu o' the premises[10]
Of homage and I know not how much tribute,
Should presently extirpate me and mine
Out of the dukedom, and confer fair Milan,
With all the honours, on my brother: whereon,
A treacherous army levied, one midnight
Fated to the purpose, did Antonio open
The gates of Milan; and, i' the dead of darkness,
The ministers for the purpose hurried thence
Me and thy crying self.
MIR.   Alack, for pity!
I, not remembering how I cried out then,
Will cry it o'er again: it is a hint
That wrings mine eyes to 't.
PROS.   Hear a little further,
And then I 'll bring thee to the present business
Which now 's upon 's; without the which, this story
Were most impertinent.
MIR.   Wherefore did they not
That hour destroy us?
PROS.   Well demanded, wench:
My tale provokes that question. Dear, they durst not,
So dear the love my people bore me; nor set
A mark so bloody on the business; but
With colours fairer painted their foul ends.
In few,[11] they hurried us aboard a bark,
Bore us some leagues to sea; where they prepared
A rotten carcass of a butt,[12] not rigg'd,
Nor tackle, sail, nor mast; the very rats
Instinctively have quit it: there they hoist us,
To cry to the sea that roar'd to us; to sigh
To the winds, whose pity, sighing back again,
Did us but loving wrong.
MIR.   Alack, what trouble
Was I then to you!

---

[10]*in lieu o' the premises*] in exchange for the conditions or stipulations.
[11]*In few*] In few words, in short.
[12]*butt*] barrel or tub; the word is contemptuously applied to an unseaworthy boat.

PROS.   O, a cherubin
    Thou wast that did preserve me. Thou didst smile,
    Infused with a fortitude from heaven,
    When I have deck'd[13] the sea with drops full salt,
    Under my burthen groan'd; which raised in me
    An undergoing stomach,[14] to bear up
    Against what should ensue.
MIR.   How came we ashore?
PROS.   By Providence divine.
    Some food we had, and some fresh water, that
    A noble Neapolitan, Gonzalo,
    Out of his charity, who being then appointed
    Master of this design, did give us, with
    Rich garments, linens, stuffs and necessaries,
    Which since have steaded much; so, of his gentleness,
    Knowing I loved my books, he furnish'd me
    From mine own library with volumes that
    I prize above my dukedom.
MIR.   Would I might
    But ever see that man!
PROS.   Now I arise: [*Resumes his mantle.*
    Sit still, and hear the last of our sea-sorrow.
    Here in this island we arrived; and here
    Have I, thy schoolmaster, made thee more profit
    Than other princess' can, that have more time
    For vainer hours, and tutors not so careful.
MIR.   Heavens thank you for 't! And now, I pray you, sir,
    For still 't is beating in my mind, your reason
    For raising this sea-storm?
PROS.   Know thus far forth.
    By accident most strange, bountiful Fortune,
    Now my dear lady, hath mine enemies
    Brought to this shore; and by my prescience
    I find my zenith[15] doth depend upon
    A most auspicious star, whose influence
    If now I court not, but omit, my fortunes
    Will ever after droop. Here cease more questions:
    Thou art inclined to sleep; 't is a good dulness,
    And give it way: I know thou canst not choose.

                        [MIRANDA *sleeps.*

---

[13]*deck'd*] sprinkled.
[14]*undergoing stomach*] enduring courage.
[15]*my zenith*] height of my fortune.

> Come away, servant, come. I am ready now.
> Approach, my Ariel, come.

Enter ARIEL.

ARI. All hail, great master! grave sir, hail! I come
To answer thy best pleasure; be 't to fly,
To swim, to dive into the fire, to ride
On the curl'd clouds, to thy strong bidding task
Ariel and all his quality.[16]
PROS.   Hast thou, spirit,
Perform'd to point[17] the tempest that I bade thee?
ARI. To every article.
I boarded the king's ship; now on the beak,[18]
Now in the waist,[19] the deck, in every cabin,
I flamed amazement:[20] sometime I 'ld divide,
And burn in many places; on the topmast,
The yards and bowsprit, would I flame distinctly,
Then meet and join. Jove's lightnings, the precursors
O' the dreadful thunder-claps, more momentary
And sight-outrunning were not: the fire and cracks
Of sulphurous roaring the most mighty Neptune
Seem to besiege, and make his bold waves tremble,
Yea, his dread trident shake.
PROS.   My brave spirit!
Who was so firm, so constant, that this coil
Would not infect his reason?
ARI.   Not a soul
But felt a fever of the mad, and play'd
Some tricks of desperation. All but mariners
Plunged in the foaming brine, and quit the vessel,
Then all afire with me: the king's son, Ferdinand,
With hair up-staring,[21] —then like reeds, not hair, —
Was the first man that leap'd; cried, "Hell is empty,
And all the devils are here."
PROS.   Why, that's my spirit!

---

[16]*all his quality*] all his profession, all his confederates.
[17]*to point*] at every point, in every detail.
[18]*the beak*] the prow.
[19]*the waist*] the midship.
[20]*I flamed amazement*] Many sailors of Shakespeare's day reported such a phenomenon as is here described. The mysterious flame, which was held to presage a wreck, was commonly called "St. Elmo's fire"; it was doubtless due to electrical disturbances of the air.
[21]*up-staring*] standing on end.

But was not this nigh shore?

ARI.   Close by, my master.

PROS.   But are they, Ariel safe?

ARI.   Not a hair perish'd;
On their sustaining garments not a blemish,
But fresher than before: and, as thou badest me,
In troops I have dispersed them 'bout the isle.
The king's son have I landed by himself;
Whom I left cooling of the air with sighs
In an odd angle of the isle, and sitting,
His arms in this sad knot.[22]

PROS.   Of the king's ship,
The mariners, say how thou hast disposed,
And all the rest o' the fleet.

ARI.   Safely in harbour
Is the king's ship; in the deep nook, where once
Thou call'dst me up at midnight to fetch dew
From the still-vex'd Bermoothes,[23] there she 's hid:
The mariners all under hatches stow'd;
Who, with a charm join'd to their suffer'd labour,
I have left asleep: and for the rest o' the fleet,
Which I dispersed, they all have met again,
And are upon the Mediterranean flote,[24]
Bound sadly home for Naples;
Supposing that they saw the king's ship wreck'd,
And his great person perish.

PROS.   Ariel, thy charge
Exactly is perform'd: but there 's more work.
What is the time o' the day?

ARI.   Past the mid season.

PROS.   At least two glasses.[25] The time 'twixt six and now
Must by us both be spent most preciously.

ARI.   Is there more toil? Since thou dost give me pains,[26]
Let me remember thee what thou hast promised,
Which is not yet perform'd me.

---

[22]*in this sad knot*] folded thus; folded arms was commonly regarded as a sign of melancholy.

[23]*still-vex'd Bermoothes*] the island of Bermudas. Originally sighted and named by the Spanish seaman Juan de Bermudez in 1515.

[24]*flote*] wave, sea.

[25]*At least two glasses*] Shakespeare would seem to mean by "two glasses" two hours (after noon). He obviously regarded seamen's sand-glasses for measuring time as hour-glasses. In point of fact, they were half-hour glasses.

[26]*give me pains*] impose tasks on me.

PROS.   How now? moody?
    What is 't thou canst demand?
ARI.   My liberty.
PROS.   Before the time be out? no more!
ARI.   I prithee,
    Remember I have done thee worthy service;
    Told thee no lies, made thee no mistakings, served
    Without or grudge or grumblings: thou didst promise
    To bate me a full year.
PROS.   Dost thou forget
    From what a torment I did free thee?
ARI.   No.
PROS.   Thou dost; and think'st it much to tread the ooze
    Of the salt deep,
    To run upon the sharp wind of the north,
    To do me business in the veins o' the earth
    When it is baked with frost.
ARI.   I do not, sir.
PROS.   Thou liest, malignant thing! Hast thou forgot
    The foul witch Sycorax, who with age and envy
    Was grown into a hoop? hast thou forgot her?
ARI.   No, sir.
PROS.   Thou hast. Where was she born? speak; tell me.
ARI.   Sir, in Argier.
PROS.   O, was she so? I must
    Once in a month recount what thou hast been,
    Which thou forget'st. This damn'd witch Sycorax,
    For mischiefs manifold, and sorceries terrible
    To enter human hearing, from Argier,[27]
    Thou know'st, was banish'd: for one thing she did
    They would not take her life. Is not this true?
ARI.   Ay, sir.
PROS.   This blue-eyed[28] hag was hither brought with child,
    And here was left by the sailors. Thou, my slave,
    As thou report'st thyself, wast then her servant;
    And, for thou wast a spirit too delicate
    To act her earthy and abhorr'd commands,
    Refusing her grand hests, she did confine thee,
    By help of her more potent ministers,
    And in her most unmitigable rage,
    Into a cloven pine; within which rift

---

[27]*Argier*] the old form of "Algiers."
[28]*blue-eyed*] with blue-ish rings round the eye.

Imprison'd thou didst painfully remain
A dozen years; within which space she died,
And left thee there; where thou didst vent thy groans
As fast as mill-wheels strike. Then was this island—
Save for the son that she did litter here,
A freckled whelp hag-born—not honour'd with
A human shape.

ARI.   Yes, Caliban her son.

PROS.   Dull thing, I say so; he, that Caliban,
Whom now I keep in service. Thou best know'st
What torment I did find thee in; thy groans
Did make wolves howl, and penetrate the breasts
Of ever-angry bears: it was a torment
To lay upon the damn'd, which Sycorax
Could not again undo: it was mine art,
When I arrived and heard thee, that made gape
The pine, and let thee out.

ARI.   I thank thee, master.

PROS.   If thou more murmur'st, I will rend an oak,
And peg thee in his knotty entrails, till
Thou hast howl'd away twelve winters.

ARI.   Pardon, master:
I will be correspondent[29] to command,
And do my spiriting gently.

PROS.   Do so; and after two days
I will discharge thee.

ARI.   That 's my noble master!
What shall I do? say what; what shall I do?

PROS.   Go make thyself like a nymph o' the sea:
Be subject to no sight but thine and mine; invisible
To every eyeball else. Go take this shape,
And hither come in 't: go, hence with diligence!   [*Exit* ARIEL.
Awake, dear heart, awake! thou hast slept well;
Awake!

MIR.   The strangeness of your story put
Heaviness in me.

PROS.   Shake it off. Come on;
We 'll visit Caliban my slave, who never
Yields us kind answer.

MIR.   'T is a villain, sir,
I do not love to look on.

PROS.   But, as 't is,

---

[29]*correspondent*] amenable.

We cannot miss[30] him: he does make our fire,
Fetch in our wood, and serves in offices
That profit us. What, ho! slave! Caliban!
Thou earth, thou! speak.

CAL. [*within.*]   There 's wood enough within.
PROS.   Come forth, I say! there 's other business for thee:
Come, thou tortoise![31] when?

Re-enter ARIEL *like a water-nymph.*

Fine apparition! My quaint[32] Ariel,
Hark in thine ear.

ARI.   My lord, it shall be done.   [*Exit.*
PROS.   Thou poisonous slave, got by the devil himself
Upon thy wicked dam, come forth!

Enter CALIBAN.

CAL.   As wicked[33] dew as e'er my mother brush'd
With raven's feather from unwholesome fen
Drop on you both! a south-west blow on ye
And blister you all o'er!
PROS.   For this, be sure, to-night thou shalt have cramps,
Side-stitches that shall pen thy breath up; urchins
Shall, for that vast of night that they may work,
All exercise on thee;[34] thou shalt be pinch'd
As thick as honeycomb, each pinch more stinging
Than bees that made 'em.
CAL.   I must eat my dinner.
This island 's mine, by Sycorax my mother,
Which thou takest from me. When thou camest first,
Thou strokedst me, and madest much of me; wouldst give me
Water with berries in 't;[35] and teach me how
To name the bigger light, and how the less,
That burn by day and night: and then I loved thee,
And show'd thee all the qualities o' th' isle,
The fresh springs, brine-pits, barren place and fertile:

[30]*miss*] do without.
[31]*thou tortoise!*] suggesting Caliban's slow gait and unwieldy form.
[32]*quaint*] ingenious.
[33]*wicked*] baneful.
[34]*urchins . . . exercise on thee*] The meaning seems to be: "goblins in the shape of hedgehogs shall, during that desolate period of the night when they are permitted to work,
practise all their torments on thee."
[35]*Water with berries in 't*] The reference seems to be to the berries of the cedar trees, out
of which shipwrecked mariners made a kind of drink.

Cursed be I that did so! All the charms
Of Sycorax, toads, beetles, bats, light on you!
For I am all the subjects that you have,
Which first was mine own king: and here you sty me
In this hard rock, whiles you do keep from me
The rest o' th' island.

PROS.   Thou most lying slave,
Whom stripes may move, not kindness! I have used thee,
Filth as thou art, with human care; and lodged thee
In mine own cell, till thou didst seek to violate
The honour of my child.

CAL.   O ho, O ho! would 't had been done!
Thou didst prevent me; I had peopled else
This isle with Calibans.

PROS.   Abhorred slave,
Which any print of goodness wilt not take,
Being capable of all ill! I pitied thee,
Took pains to make thee speak, taught thee each hour
One thing or other: when thou didst not, savage,
Know thine own meaning, but wouldst gabble like
A thing most brutish, I endow'd thy purposes
With words that made them known. But thy vile race,
Though thou didst learn, had that in 't which good natures
Could not abide to be with; therefore wast thou
Deservedly confined into this rock,
Who hadst served more than a prison.

CAL.   You taught me language; and my profit on 't
Is, I know how to curse. The red plague rid you
For learning me your language!

PROS.   Hag-seed, hence!
Fetch us in fuel; and be quick, thou 'rt best,
To answer other business. Shrug'st thou, malice?
If thou neglect'st, or dost unwillingly
What I command, I 'll rack thee with old cramps,
Fill all thy bones with aches, make thee roar,
That beasts shall tremble at thy din.

CAL.   No, pray thee.
[*Aside.*] I must obey: his art is of such power,
It would control my dam's god, Setebos,[36]
And make a vassal of him.

PROS.   So, slave; hence!   [*Exit* CALIBAN.

---

[36]*Setebos*] the greatest of the devils in Patagonian worship (from an early account of
Magellan's voyage).

Re-enter ARIEL, *invisible, playing and singing;* FERDINAND *following*.

ARIEL'S song.

Come unto these yellow sands,
 And then take hands:
Courtsied when you have and kiss'd
 The wild waves whist:[37]
Foot it featly here and there;
And, sweet sprites, the burthen bear.
  Hark, hark!
 Burthen [*dispersedly*]. Bow-wow.
ARI. The watch-dogs bark:
 Burthen [*dispersedly*]. Bow-wow.
ARI. Hark, hark! I hear
 The strain of strutting chanticleer
 Cry, Cock-a-diddle-dow.[38]

FER. Where should this music be? i' th' air or th' earth?
It sounds no more: and, sure, it waits upon
Some god o' th' island. Sitting on a bank,
Weeping again the king my father's wreck,
This music crept by me upon the waters,
Allaying both their fury and my passion
With its sweet air: thence I have follow'd it,
Or it hath drawn me rather. But 't is gone.
No, it begins again.

ARIEL *sings*.

Full fathom five thy father lies;
 Of his bones are coral made;
Those are pearls that were his eyes:
 Nothing of him that doth fade,
But doth suffer a sea-change
Into something rich and strange.
Sea-nymphs hourly ring his knell:
     Burthen: Ding-dong.
ARI. Hark! now I hear them,—Ding-dong, bell.

FER. The ditty does remember my drown'd father.
This is no mortal business, nor no sound
That the earth owes:—I hear it now above me.

---

[37]*Courtsied . . . whist*] When you have courtsied and kissed the wild waves into silence.
[38]*Cry, Cock-a-diddle-dow*] This line has been sometimes printed as a stage direction, a change worth considering.

PROS.   The fringed curtains of thine eye advance,[39]
  And say what thou seest yond.
MIR.   What is 't? a spirit?
  Lord, how it looks about! Believe me, sir,
  It carries a brave form. But 't is a spirit.
PROS.   No, wench; it eats and sleeps and hath such senses
  As we have, such. This gallant which thou seest
  Was in the wreck; and, but he 's something stain'd
  With grief, that 's beauty's canker, thou mightst call him
  A goodly person: he hath lost his fellows,
  And strays about to find 'em.
MIR.   I might call him
  A thing divine; for nothing natural
  I ever saw so noble.
PROS.   [*Aside.*] It goes on, I see,
  As my soul prompts it. Spirit, fine spirit! I 'll free thee
  Within two days for this.
FER.   Most sure, the goddess
  On whom these airs attend! Vouchsafe my prayer
  May know if you remain upon this island;
  And that you will some good instruction give
  How I may bear me here: my prime request,
  Which I do last pronounce, is, O you wonder!
  If you be maid or no?
MIR.   No wonder, sir;
  But certainly a maid.
FER.   My language! heavens!
  I am the best of them that speak this speech,
  Were I but where 't is spoken.
PROS.   How? the best?
  What wert thou, if the King of Naples heard thee?
FER.   A single thing, as I am now, that wonders
  To hear thee speak of Naples. He does hear me;
  And that he does I weep: myself am Naples,
  Who with mine eyes, never since at ebb, beheld
  The king my father wreck'd.
MIR.   Alack, for mercy!
FER.   Yes, faith, and all his lords; the Duke of Milan
  And his brave son[40] being twain.

---

[39]*advance*] raise, lift.
[40]*his brave son*] No other reference is made to any son of the Duke Antonio of Milan.
 This reference is probably a survival from the unknown story whence Shakespeare
 borrowed his plot.

PROS.   [*Aside.*] The Duke of Milan
        And his more braver daughter could control thee,
        If now 't were fit to do 't. At the first sight
        They have changed eyes.[41] Delicate Ariel,
        I 'll set thee free for this.   [*To* FER.] A word, good sir;
        I fear you have done yourself some wrong: a word.
MIR.   Why speaks my father so ungently? This
        Is the third man that e'er I saw; the first
        That e'er I sigh'd for: pity move my father
        To be inclined my way!
FER.   O, if a virgin,
        And your affection not gone forth, I 'll make you
        The queen of Naples.
PROS.   Soft, sir! one word more.
        [*Aside.*] They are both in either's powers: but this swift business
        I must uneasy make, lest too light winning
        Make the prize light.   [*To* FER.] One word more; I charge thee
        That thou attend me: thou dost here usurp
        The name thou owest not; and hast put thyself
        Upon this island as a spy, to win it
        From me, the lord on 't.
FER.   No, as I am a man.
MIR.   There 's nothing ill can dwell in such a temple:
        If the ill spirit have so fair a house,
        Good things will strive to dwell with 't.
PROS.   Follow me.
        Speak not you for him; he 's a traitor. Come;
        I 'll manacle thy neck and feet together:
        Sea-water shalt thou drink; thy food shall be
        The fresh-brook muscles, wither'd roots, and husks
        Wherein the acorn cradled. Follow.
FER.   No;
        I will resist such entertainment till
        Mine enemy has more power.
                          [*Draws, and is charmed from moving.*
MIR.   O dear father,
        Make not too rash a trial of him, for
        He 's gentle, and not fearful.[42]

---

[41]*changed eyes*] fallen in love.
[42]*He 's gentle . . . fearful*] He 's of gentle birth, and not formidable.

PROS.   What! I say,
   My foot my tutor?[43] Put thy sword up, traitor;
   Who makest a show, but darest not strike, thy conscience
   Is so possess'd with guilt: come from thy ward;[44]
   For I can here disarm thee with this stick
   And make thy weapon drop.
MIR.   Beseech you, father.
PROS.   Hence! hang not on my garments.
MIR.   Sir, have pity;
   I 'll be his surety.
PROS.   Silence! one word more
   Shall make me chide thee, if not hate thee. What!
   An advocate for an impostor! hush!
   Thou think'st there is no more such shapes as he,
   Having seen but him and Caliban: foolish wench!
   To the most of men this is a Caliban,
   And they to him are angels.
MIR.   My affections
   Are, then, most humble; I have no ambition
   To see a goodlier man.
PROS.   Come on; obey:
   Thy nerves[45] are in their infancy again,
   And have no vigour in them.
FER.   So they are:
   My spirits, as in a dream, are all bound up.
   My father's loss, the weakness which I feel,
   The wreck of all my friends, nor this man's threats,
   To whom I am subdued, are but light to me,
   Might I but through my prison once a day
   Behold this maid: all corners else o' th' earth
   Let liberty make use of; space enough
   Have I in such a prison.
PROS.   [*Aside.*] It works. [*To* FER.] Come on.
   Thou hast done well, fine Ariel! [*To* FER.] Follow me.
   [*To* ARI.] Hark what thou else shalt do me.
MIR.   Be of comfort;
   My father 's of a better nature, sir,
   Than he appears by speech: this is unwonted
   Which now came from him.

---

[43]*My foot my tutor?*] A proverbial phrase meaning "Shall an inferior object exercise authority over me?"
[44]*come from thy ward*] give up that posture of defence (which does not alarm me).
[45]*nerves*] sinews.

PROS.   Thou shalt be as free
    . As mountain winds: but then exactly do
     All points of my command.
ARI.   To the syllable.
PROS.   Come, follow. Speak not for him.   [*Exeunt.*

ACT II.

SCENE I. *Another Part of the Island.*

Enter ALONSO, SEBASTIAN, ANTONIO, GONZALO, ADRIAN, FRANCISCO,
and others.

GON. Beseech you, sir, be merry; you have cause,
So have we all, of joy; for our escape
Is much beyond our loss. Our hint[1] of woe
Is common; every day, some sailor's wife,
The masters of some merchant,[2] and the merchant,
Have just our theme of woe; but for the miracle,
I mean our preservation, few in millions
Can speak like us: then wisely, good sir, weigh
Our sorrow with our comfort.

ALON.   Prithee, peace.

SEB. He receives comfort like cold porridge.

ANT. The visitor will not give him o'er so.[3]

SEB. Look, he 's winding up the watch of his wit; by and by it will
strike.

GON. Sir,—

SEB. One: tell.[4]

GON. When every grief is entertain'd that 's offer'd,
Comes to the entertainer—

SEB. A dollar.[5]

---

[1]*hint*] theme.
[2]*merchant*] merchant-vessel.
[3]*The visitor . . . so*] Gonzalo is likened to one who visits the sick.
[4]*tell*] count.
[5]*A dollar*] Sebastian affects to take "entertainer" in the sense of "innkeeper," to whom
dollars or coins "come" naturally. Gonzalo in reply punningly mistakes *dollar*, the
coin, for *dolour*, grief.

GON. Dolour comes to him, indeed: you have spoken truer than you
      purposed.
SEB. You have taken it wiselier than I meant you should.
GON. Therefore, my lord,—
ANT. Fie, what a spendthrift is he of his tongue!
ALON. I prithee, spare.
GON. Well, I have done: but yet,—
SEB. He will be talking.
ANT. Which, of he or Adrian,[6] for a good wager, first begins to crow?
SEB. The old cock.
ANT. The cockerel.
SEB. Done. The wager?
ANT. A laughter.
SEB. A match!
ADR. Though this island seem to be desert,—
SEB. Ha, ha, ha!—So, you 're paid.[7]
ADR. Uninhabitable, and almost inaccessible,—
SEB. Yet,—
ADR. Yet,—
ANT. He could not miss 't.[8]
ADR. It must needs be of subtle, tender and delicate temperance.[9]
ANT. Temperance was a delicate wench.
SEB. Ay, and a subtle; as he most learnedly delivered.
ADR. The air breathes upon us here most sweetly.
SEB. As if it had lungs, and rotten ones.
ANT. Or as 't were perfumed by a fen.
GON. Here is everything advantageous to life.
ANT. True; save means to live.
SEB. Of that there 's none, or little.
GON. How lush and lusty the grass looks! how green!
ANT. The ground, indeed, is tawny.
SEB. With an eye of green[10] in 't.
ANT. He misses not much.
SEB. No; he doth but mistake the truth totally.
GON. But the rarity of it is,—which is indeed almost beyond credit,—
SEB. As many vouched rarities are.

[6]*Which, of he or Adrian*] Which of the two, he or Adrian?
[7]*A laughter . . . paid*] Laughter is the wager. The one who crows or speaks first wins the
   bet, and the loser is to pay with a laugh. Adrian speaks first; Sebastian loses the wager
   and pays his adversary with "Ha, ha, ha!"
[8]*He could not miss 't*] He could not miss the word "yet."
[9]*temperance*] temperature. In the next line the word is used in its more ordinary sense
   of one of the cardinal virtues.
[10]*an eye of green*] a shade or tinge of green.

GON. That our garments, being, as they were, drenched in the sea, hold, notwithstanding, their freshness and glosses, being rather new-dyed than stained with salt water.

ANT. If but one of his pockets could speak, would it not say he lies?

SEB. Ay, or very falsely pocket up his report.

GON. Methinks our garments are now as fresh as when we put them on first in Afric, at the marriage of the king's fair daughter Claribel to the King of Tunis.

SEB. 'T was a sweet marriage, and we prosper well in our return.

ADR. Tunis was never graced before with such a paragon to their queen.

GON. Not since widow Dido's time.

ANT. Widow! a pox o' that! How came that widow in? widow Dido!

SEB. What if he had said "widower Æneas" too?
Good Lord, how you take it!

ADR. "Widow Dido" said you? you make me study of that: she was of Carthage, not of Tunis.

GON. This Tunis, sir, was Carthage.

ADR. Carthage?

GON. I assure you, Carthage.

ANT. His word is more than the miraculous harp.[11]

SEB. He hath raised the wall, and houses too.

ANT. What impossible matter will he make easy next?

SEB. I think he will carry this island home in his pocket, and give it his son for an apple.

ANT. And, sowing the kernels of it in the sea, bring forth more islands.

GON. Ay.

ANT. Why, in good time.

GON. Sir, we were talking that our garments seem now as fresh as when we were at Tunis at the marriage of your daughter, who is now queen.

ANT. And the rarest that e'er came there.

SEB. Bate, I beseech you, widow Dido.

ANT. O, widow Dido! ay, widow Dido.

GON. Is not, sir, my doublet as fresh as the first day I wore it? I mean, in a sort.[12]

ANT. That sort was well fished for.

GON. When I wore it at your daughter's marriage?

ALON. You cram these words into mine ears against

---

[11]*the miraculous harp*] The reference is probably to the music of Apollo's lyre, which, according to Ovid's *Heroides*, miraculously called into being the walls and towers of Troy.

[12]*in a sort*] comparatively.

The stomach of my sense.[13] Would I had never
Married my daughter there! for, coming thence,
My son is lost, and, in my rate,[14] she too,
Who is so far from Italy removed
I ne'er again shall see her. O thou mine heir
Of Naples and of Milan, what strange fish
Hath made his meal on thee?

FRAN.   Sir, he may live:
I saw him beat the surges under him,
And ride upon their backs; he trod the water,
Whose enmity he flung aside, and breasted
The surge most swoln that met him; his bold head
'Bove the contentious waves he kept, and oar'd
Himself with his good arms in lusty stroke
To the shore, that o'er his wave-worn basis[15] bow'd,
As stooping to relieve him: I not doubt
He came alive to land.

ALON.   No, no, he 's gone.

SEB.   Sir, you may thank yourself for this great loss,
That would not bless our Europe with your daughter,
But rather lose her to an African;
Where she, at least, is banish'd from your eye,
Who hath cause to wet the grief on 't.

ALON.   Prithee, peace.

SEB.   You were kneel'd to, and importuned otherwise,
By all of us; and the fair soul herself
Weigh'd between loathness and obedience, at
Which end o' the beam should bow. We have lost your son,
I fear, for ever: Milan and Naples have
Mo widows in them of this business' making
Than we bring men to comfort them:
The fault 's your own.

ALON.   So is the dear'st[16] o' the loss.

GON.   My lord Sebastian,
The truth you speak doth lack some gentleness,
And time to speak it in: you rub the sore,
When you should bring the plaster.

---

[13]*against The stomach of my sense*] without my wishing to hear them, contrary to the appetite of my feelings.

[14]*in my rate*] in my reckoning or opinion.

[15]*his wave-worn basis*] the wave-worn base or ground of the shore; "his" is the common form of "its."

[16]*dear'st*] greatest, bitterest.

SEB.   Very well.
ANT.   And most chirurgeonly.[17]
GON.   It is foul weather in us all, good sir,
        When you are cloudy.
SEB.   Foul weather?
ANT.   Very foul.
GON.   Had I plantation[18] of this isle, my lord, —
ANT.   He 'ld sow 't with nettle-seed.
SEB.   Or docks, or mallows.
GON.   And were the king on 't, what would I do?
SEB.   'Scape being drunk for want of wine.
GON.   I' the commonwealth I would by contraries
        Execute all things; for no kind of traffic
        Would I admit; no name of magistrate;
        Letters should not be known; riches, poverty,
        And use of service, none; contract, succession,[19]
        Bourn, bound of land, tilth, vineyard, none;
        No use of metal, corn, or wine, or oil;
        No occupation; all men idle, all;
        And women too, but innocent and pure;
        No sovereignty; —
SEB.   Yet he would be king on 't.
ANT.   The latter end of his commonwealth forgets the beginning.
GON.   All things in common nature should produce
        Without sweat or endeavour: treason, felony,
        Sword, pike, knife, gun, or need of any engine,[20]
        Would I not have; but nature should bring forth,
        Of its own kind, all foison,[21] all abundance,
        To feed my innocent people.
SEB.   No marrying 'mong his subjects?
ANT.   None, man; all idle; whores and knaves.
GON.   I would with such perfection govern, sir,
        To excel the golden age.
SEB.   'Save his majesty!
ANT.   Long live Gonzalo!
GON.   And, — do you mark me, sir?
ALON.   Prithee, no more: thou dost talk nothing to me.

[17]*chirurgeonly*] surgeon-like.
[18]*plantation*] colonisation. A "plantation" was also the ordinary word at the time for "a colony."
[19]*succession*] tenure of property by inheritance.
[20]*engine*] that is, any engine of war.
[21]*foison*] harvest.

GON.   I do well believe your highness; and did it to minister occasion
to these gentlemen, who are of such sensible and nimble lungs
that they always use to laugh at nothing.

ANT.   'T was you we laughed at.

GON.   Who in this kind of merry fooling am nothing to you: so you
may continue, and laugh at nothing still.

ANT.   What a blow was there given!

SEB.   An it had not fallen flat-long.[22]

GON.   You are gentlemen of brave mettle; you would lift the moon
out of her sphere, if she would continue in it five weeks without
changing.

Enter ARIEL *(invisible) playing solemn music.*

SEB.   We would so, and then go a bat-fowling.[23]

ANT.   Nay, good my lord, be not angry.

GON.   No, I warrant you; I will not adventure my discretion so
weakly.[24] Will you laugh me asleep, for I am very heavy?

ANT.   Go sleep, and hear us.[25]

All sleep except ALON., SEB., *and* ANT.

ALON.   What, all so soon asleep! I wish mine eyes
Would, with themselves, shut up my thoughts: I find
They are inclined to do so.

SEB.   Please you, sir,
Do not omit the heavy offer of it:[26]
It seldom visits sorrow; when it doth,
It is a comforter.

ANT.   We two, my lord,
Will guard your person while you take your rest,
And watch your safety.

ALON.   Thank you. — Wondrous heavy.

ALONSO *sleeps. Exit* ARIEL.

SEB.   What a strange drowsiness possesses them!

ANT.   It is the quality o' the climate.

---

[22]*fallen flat-long*] hit with the flat of the sword (instead of with the edge).

[23]*bat-fowling*] catching birds by night, by suddenly lighting a fire about them, and then
batting or cudgelling them as they endeavour to escape.

[24]*I will not . . . weakly*] I will not risk my character for discretion by conduct so weak.

[25]*Go sleep, and hear us*] laugh. Gonzalo suggests in the previous line that laughter will
send him to sleep. Antonio accepts the suggestion that laughter will keep him slum-
bering.

[26]*omit the heavy offer of it*] neglect the offer of heavy sleep.

SEB.   Why
    Doth it not then our eyelids sink? I find not
    Myself disposed to sleep.
ANT.   Nor I; my spirits are nimble.
    They fell together all, as by consent;
    They dropp'd, as by a thunder-stroke. What might,
    Worthy Sebastian?—O, what might?—No more:—
    And yet methinks I see it in thy face,
    What thou shouldst be: the occasion speaks thee;[27] and
    My strong imagination sees a crown
    Dropping upon thy head.
SEB.   What, art thou waking?
ANT.   Do you not hear me speak?
SEB.   I do; and surely
    It is a sleepy language, and thou speak'st
    Out of thy sleep. What is it thou didst say?
    This is a strange repose, to be asleep
    With eyes wide open; standing, speaking, moving,
    And yet so fast asleep.
ANT.   Noble Sebastian,
    Thou let'st thy fortune sleep—die, rather; wink'st
    Whiles thou art waking.[28]
SEB.   Thou dost snore distinctly;
    There 's meaning in thy snores.
ANT.   I am more serious than my custom: you
    Must be so too, if heed me; which to do
    Trebles thee o'er.[29]
SEB.   Well, I am standing water.[30]
ANT.   I 'll teach you how to flow.
SEB.   Do so: to ebb
    Hereditary sloth instructs me.
ANT.   O,
    If you but knew how you the purpose cherish
    Whiles thus you mock it! how, in stripping it,
    You more invest it![31] Ebbing men,[32] indeed,
    Most often do so near the bottom run
    By their own fear or sloth.

---

[27]*speaks thee*] proclaims thy destiny.
[28]*wink'st Whiles thou art waking*] closest thine eyes whilst thou art awake.
[29]*Trebles thee o'er*] Makes thee thrice what thou now art.
[30]*standing water*] neither flowing nor ebbing, passive.
[31]*how, in stripping it, . . . invest it*] how, in stripping the purpose of obscurity, you invest
    it with the more approval.
[32]*Ebbing men*] men whose fortunes are declining.

SEB.   Prithee, say on:
    The setting of thine eye[33] and cheek proclaim
    A matter from thee; and a birth, indeed,
    Which throes thee much to yield.[34]
ANT.   Thus, sir:
    Although this lord of weak remembrance,[35] this,
    Who shall be of as little memory
    When he is earth'd, hath here almost persuaded,—
    For he 's a spirit of persuasion, only
    Professes to persuade,[36]—the king his son 's alive,
    'T is as impossible that he 's undrown'd
    As he that sleeps here swims.
SEB.   I have no hope
    That he 's undrown'd.
ANT.   O, out of that "no hope"
    What great hope have you! no hope that way is
    Another way so high a hope that even
    Ambition cannot pierce a wink beyond,
    But doubt discovery there.[37] Will you grant with me
    That Ferdinand is drown'd?
SEB.   He 's gone.
ANT.   Then, tell me,
    Who 's the next heir of Naples?
SEB.   Claribel:
ANT.   She that is queen of Tunis; she that dwells
    Ten leagues beyond man's life;[38] she that from Naples
    Can have no note, unless the sun were post,—
    The man i' the moon 's too slow,—till new-born chins
    Be rough and razorable; she that from whom
    We all were sea-swallow'd, though some cast again,
    And by that destiny, to perform an act
    Whereof what 's past is prologue; what to come,
    In yours and my discharge.[39]
SEB.   What stuff is this! How say you?
    'T is true, my brother's daughter 's queen of Tunis;

[33]*The setting of thine eye*] the fixed expression.
[34]*throes . . . yield*] pains thee greatly to utter.
[35]*weak remembrance*] feeble memory.
[36]*only . . . persuade*] persuading is his only profession.
[37]*"no hope" . . . discovery*] abandonment of hope of the prince's safety makes way, from another point of view, for so lofty a design that even ambition cannot reach a jot further, cannot but be doubtful of discovering anything beyond.
[38]*Ten leagues beyond man's life*] a greater distance than man could travel in a lifetime.
[39]*In yours . . . discharge*] depends on what you and I will do.

So is she heir of Naples; 'twixt which regions
There is some space.
ANT.   A space whose every cubit
Seems to cry out, "How shall that Claribel
Measure us back to Naples? Keep in Tunis,[40]
And let Sebastian wake." Say, this were death
That now hath seized them; why, they were no worse
Than now they are. There be that can rule Naples
As well as he that sleeps; lords that can prate
As amply and unnecessarily
As this Gonzalo; I myself could make
A chough of as deep chat.[41] O, that you bore
The mind that I do! what a sleep were this
For your advancement! Do you understand me?
SEB.   Methinks I do.
ANT.   And how does your content
Tender your own good fortune?[42]
SEB.   I remember
You did supplant your brother Prospero.
ANT.   True:
And look how well my garments sit upon me;
Much feater[43] than before: my brother's servants
Were then my fellows; now they are my men.
SEB.   But, for your conscience.
ANT.   Ay, sir; where lies that? if 't were a kibe,
'T would put me to my slipper: but I feel not
This deity in my bosom: twenty consciences,
That stand 'twixt me and Milan, candied be they,
And melt,[44] ere they molest! Here lies your brother,
No better than the earth he lies upon,
If he were that which now he 's like, that 's dead;
Whom I, with this obedient steel, three inches of it,
Can lay to bed for ever; whiles you, doing thus,
To the perpetual wink[45] for aye might put
This ancient morsel, this Sir Prudence, who
Should not upbraid our course. For all the rest,

---

[40]*Measure . . . Tunis*] Follow us back to Naples? Let Claribel stay in Tunis.
[41]*A chough . . . chat*] A chough or jackdaw able to talk as profoundly.
[42]*how does your content . . . fortune?*] are you content or willing to look after your own
good fortune?
[43]*feater*] more featly, gracefully.
[44]*candied . . . melt*] let them congeal and melt away, as congealed things must.
[45]*perpetual wink*] eternal sleep of death.

They 'll take suggestion[46] as a cat laps milk;
They 'll tell the clock to any business that
We say befits the hour.
SEB.   Thy case, dear friend,
Shall be my precedent; as thou got'st Milan,
I 'll come by Naples. Draw thy sword: one stroke
Shall free thee from the tribute which thou payest;
And I the king shall love thee.
ANT.   Draw together;
And when I rear my hand, do you the like
To fall it on Gonzalo.
SEB.   O, but one word.   [They talk apart.

Re-enter ARIEL invisible.

ARI.   My master through his art foresees the danger
That you, his friend, are in; and sends me forth,—
For else his project dies,—to keep them living.[47]
                              [Sings in GONZALO's ear.

While you here do snoring lie,
Open-eyed conspiracy
His time doth take.
If of life you keep a care,
Shake off slumber, and beware:
Awake, awake!

ANT.   Then let us both be sudden.
GON.   Now, good angels
Preserve the king!   [They wake.
ALON.   Why, how now? ho, awake!—why are you drawn?[48]
Wherefore this ghastly looking?
GON.   What 's the matter?
SEB.   Whiles we stood here securing your repose,
Even now, we heard a hollow burst of bellowing
Like bulls, or rather lions: did 't not wake you?
It struck mine ear most terribly.
ALON.   I heard nothing.
ANT.   O, 't was a din to fright a monster's ear,
To make an earthquake! sure, it was the roar
Of a whole herd of lions.

[46]take suggestion] succumb to temptation.
[47]to keep them living] "Them" refers to Gonzalo and Alonso. Ariel is half apostrophis-
ing Gonzalo and half talking to himself.
[48]are you drawn?] are your swords drawn?

ALON.   Heard you this, Gonzalo?
GON.   Upon mine honour, sir, I heard a humming,
      And that a strange one too, which did awake me:
      I shaked you, sir, and cried: as mine eyes open'd,
      I saw their weapons drawn:—there was a noise,
      That 's verily. 'T is best we stand upon our guard,
      Or that we quit this place: let 's draw our weapons.
ALON.   Lead off this ground; and let 's make further search
      For my poor son.
GON.   Heavens keep him from these beasts!
      For he is, sure, i' th' island.
ALON.   Lead away.
ARI.   Prospero my lord shall know what I have done:
      So, king, go safely on to seek thy son.   [*Exeunt.*

SCENE II. *Another Part of the Island.*

Enter CALIBAN *with a burden of wood. A noise of thunder heard.*

CAL.   All the infections that the sun sucks up
      From bogs, fens, flats, on Prosper fall, and make him
      By inch-meal[1] a disease! His spirits hear me,
      And yet I needs must curse. But they 'll nor pinch,
      Fright me with urchin-shows,[2] pitch me i' the mire,
      Nor lead me, like a firebrand, in the dark
      Out of my way, unless he bid 'em: but
      For every trifle are they set upon me;
      Sometimes like apes, that mow[3] and chatter at me,
      And after bite me; then like hedgehogs, which
      Lie tumbling in my barefoot way, and mount
      Their pricks at my footfall; sometimes am I
      All wound with adders, who with cloven tongues
      Do hiss me into madness.

Enter TRINCULO.

                     Lo, now, lo!
      Here comes a spirit of his, and to torment me
      For bringing wood in slowly. I 'll fall flat;
      Perchance he will not mind me.

[1] *By inch-meal*] By inches, piecemeal.
[2] *urchin-shows*] goblins in the shape of hedgehogs.
[3] *mow*] make grimaces.

TRIN.   Here 's neither bush nor shrub, to bear off any weather at all,[4]
and another storm brewing; I hear it sing i' the wind: yond same
black cloud, yond huge one, looks like a foul bombard[5] that would
shed his liquor. If it should thunder as it did before, I know not
where to hide my head: yond same cloud cannot choose but fall
by pailfuls. What have we here? a man or a fish? dead or alive? A
fish: he smells like a fish; a very ancient and fish-like smell; a kind
of not of the newest Poor-John.[6] A strange fish! Were I in England
now, as once I was, and had but this fish painted, not a holiday
fool there but would give a piece of silver: there would this monster make a man;[7] any strange beast there makes a man: when they
will not give a doit to relieve a lame beggar, they will lay out ten
to see a dead Indian.[8] Legged like a man! and his fins like arms!
Warm o' my troth! I do not let loose my opinion; hold it no longer:
this is no fish, but an islander, that hath lately suffered by a thun-
derbolt. [*Thunder.*] Alas, the storm is come again! my best way is
to creep under his gaberdine;[9] there is no other shelter hereabout:
misery acquaints a man with strange bed-fellows. I will here
shroud till the dregs of the storm be past.

Enter STEPHANO, *singing: a bottle in his hand.*

STE.   I shall no more to sea, to sea,
                            Here shall I die a-shore,—

This is a very scurvy tune to sing at a man's funeral: well, here 's
my comfort.   [*Drinks.*

[*Sings.*   The master, the swabber, the boatswain, and I,
                            The gunner, and his mate,
                   Loved Mall, Meg, and Marian, and Margery,
                            But none of us cared for Kate;
                            For she had a tongue with a tang,
                            Would cry to a sailor, Go hang!
                   She loved not the savour of tar nor of pitch;
                   Yet a tailor might scratch her where'er she did itch.
                            Then, to sea, boys, and let her go hang!

[4]*bear off . . . at all*] bear the fury of the storm, and so keep it off me.
[5]*bombard*] a large tankard or drinking vessel.
[6]*Poor-John*] a coarse fish; the name is often applied to "hake," which was eaten salted
   and dried.
[7]*make a man*] make a man's fortune.
[8]*a dead Indian*] Several American Indians were brought home by explorers of the New
   World during Shakespeare's lifetime, and excited vast popular curiosity. The deaths of
   several of these visitors are recorded, and the body of one of them was probably ex-
   hibited to the public shortly before this play was performed.
[9]*gaberdine*] a coarse outer cloak.

This is a scurvy tune too: but here 's my comfort.   [*Drinks.*

CAL.   Do not torment me:—O!

STE.   What 's the matter? Have we devils here? Do you put tricks upon 's with salvages and men of Ind,[10] ha? I have not scaped drowning, to be afeard now of your four legs; for it hath been said, As proper a man as ever went on four legs[11] cannot make him give grounds; and it shall be said so again, while Stephano breathes at nostrils.

CAL.   The spirit torments me:—O!

STE.   This is some monster of the isle with four legs, who hath got, as I take it, an ague. Where the devil should he learn our language? I will give him some relief, if it be but for that. If I can recover him, and keep him tame, and get to Naples with him, he 's a present for any emperor that ever trod on neat's-leather.[12]

CAL.   Do not torment me, prithee; I 'll bring my wood home faster.

STE.   He 's in his fit now, and does not talk after the wisest. He shall taste of my bottle: if he have never drunk wine afore, it will go near to remove his fit. If I can recover him, and keep him tame, I will not take too much for him;[13] he shall pay for him that hath him, and that soundly.

CAL.   Thou dost me yet but little hurt; thou wilt anon, I know it by thy trembling:[14] now Prosper works upon thee.

STE.   Come on your ways; open your mouth; here is that which will give language to you, cat:[15] open your mouth; this will shake your shaking, I can tell you, and that soundly: you cannot tell who 's your friend: open your chaps again.

TRIN.   I should know that voice: it should be—but he is drowned; and these are devils:—O defend me!

STE.   Four legs and two voices,—a most delicate monster! His forward voice, now, is to speak well of his friend; his backward voice is to utter foul speeches and to detract. If all the wine in my bottle will recover him, I will help his ague. Come:—Amen! I will pour some in thy other mouth.

TRIN.   Stephano!

---

[10]*salvages and men of Ind*] Both America and Asia were known indifferently as "Ind" or "India" in Shakespeare's day, though "West Indies" was a title more correctly borne by America, as "East Indies" was the juster name of Southern Asia. "A man of Ind" was the term frequently applied to an American Indian.

[11]*a man . . . on four legs*] often said of a man on crutches.

[12]*neat's-leather*] cowhide or calf's skin.

[13]*I will not take too much for him*] an ironical way of saying "I will take all I can get."

[14]*trembling*] a recognised sign of demoniacal possession.

[15]*cat*] Cf. the proverb "Good liquor will *make a cat speak.*"

STE.   Doth thy other mouth call me? Mercy, mercy! This is a devil, and no monster: I will leave him; I have no long spoon.[16]

TRIN.   Stephano! If thou beest Stephano, touch me, and speak to me; for I am Trinculo,—be not afeard,—thy good friend Trinculo.

STE.   If thou beest Trinculo, come forth: I 'll pull thee by the lesser legs: if any be Trinculo's legs, these are they. Thou art very Trinculo indeed! How camest thou to be the siege of this moon-calf?[17] can he vent Trinculos?

TRIN.   I took him to be killed with a thunder-stroke. But art thou not drowned, Stephano? I hope, now, thou art not drowned. Is the storm overblown? I hid me under the dead moon-calf's gaberdine for fear of the storm. And art thou living, Stephano? O Stephano, two Neapolitans scaped!

STE.   Prithee, do not turn me about; my stomach is not constant.[18]

CAL.   [Aside.] These be fine things, an if they be not sprites.
That 's a brave god, and bears celestial liquor:
I will kneel to him.

STE.   How didst thou 'scape? How camest thou hither? swear, by this bottle, how thou camest hither. I escaped upon a butt of sack, which the sailors heaved o'erboard, by this bottle! which I made of the bark of a tree with mine own hands, since I was cast ashore.

CAL.   I 'll swear, upon that bottle, to be thy true subject; for the liquor is not earthly.

STE.   Here; swear, then, how thou escapedst.

TRIN.   Swum ashore, man, like a duck: I can swim like a duck, I 'll be sworn.

STE.   Here, kiss the book.[19] Though thou canst swim like a duck, thou art made like a goose.

TRIN.   O Stephano, hast any more of this?

STE.   The whole butt, man: my cellar is in a rock by the sea-side, where my wine is hid. How now, moon-calf! How does thine ague?

CAL.   Hast thou not dropp'd from heaven?

STE.   Out o' the moon, I do assure thee: I was the man i' the moon when time was.

---

[16]*I have no long spoon*] In Act IV, Scene iii, of *Comedy of Errors*, Shakespeare wrote: "Marry, he must have a long spoon that must eat with the devil."

[17]*the siege of this moon-calf*] the seat of this abortion (misshapen through lunar influence).

[18]*not constant*]unsteady.

[19]*kiss the book*] Stephano puts the bottle to Trinculo's lips.

CAL.   I have seen thee in her, and I do adore thee: my mistress show'd
me thee, and thy dog, and thy bush.[20]

STE.   Come, swear to that; kiss the book: I will furnish it anon with
new contents: swear.

TRIN.   By this good light, this is a very shallow monster! I afeard of
him! A very weak monster! The man i' the moon! A most poor
credulous monster! Well drawn,[21] monster, in good sooth!

CAL.   I 'll show thee every fertile inch o' th' island; and I will kiss thy
foot: I prithee, be my god.

TRIN.   By this light, a most perfidious and drunken monster! when 's
god 's asleep, he 'll rob his bottle.

CAL.   I 'll kiss thy foot; I 'll swear myself thy subject.

STE.   Come on, then; down, and swear.

TRIN.   I shall laugh myself to death at this puppy-headed monster. A
most scurvy monster! I could find in my heart to beat him,—

STE.   Come, kiss.·

TRIN.   But that the poor monster 's in drink. An abominable monster!

CAL.   I 'll show thee the best springs; I 'll pluck thee berries;
I 'll fish for thee, and get thee wood enough.
A plague upon the tyrant that I serve!
I 'll bear him no more sticks, but follow thee,
Thou wondrous man.

TRIN.   A most ridiculous monster, to make a wonder of a poor
drunkard!

CAL.   I prithee, let me bring thee where crabs[22] grow;
And I with my long nails will dig thee pig-nuts;[23]
Show thee a jay's nest, and instruct thee how
To snare the nimble marmoset;[24] I 'll bring thee
To clustering filberts, and sometimes I 'll get thee
Young scamels[25] form the rock. Wilt thou go with me?

STE.   I prithee now, lead the way, without any more talking. Trinculo,
the king and all our company else being drowned, we will inherit
here: here; bear my bottle: fellow Trinculo, we 'll fill him by and
by again.

CAL.   *sings drunkenly.*]   Farewell, master; farewell, farewell!

---

[20]*thy dog, and thy bush*] allusion to the superstition that the man in the moon has a dog
and a thorn bush.

[21]*Well drawn*] Heartily quaffed.

[22]*crabs*] crab-apples.

[23]*pig-nuts*] the country name of earth chestnuts, which grow underground.

[24]*marmoset*] a kind of ape or baboon now only indigenous to South America, but found
according to medieval travellers in many parts of Asia.

[25]*scamels*] The meaning of the word is uncertain. Some suggest *sea-gull* and *sea-owl*.

TRIN.   A howling monster; a drunken monster!

CAL.   No more dams I 'll make for fish;[26]
                        Nor fetch in firing
                        At requiring;
                    Nor scrape trencher, nor wash dish:
                        'Ban, 'Ban, Cacaliban
                        Has a new master:—get a new man.[27]

        Freedom, hey-day! hey-day, freedom! freedom, hey-day, freedom!
STE.   O brave monster! Lead the way.   [*Exeunt*.

---

[26]*No more dams . . . fish*] a reference to artificial weirs or dams, built to provide supplies
of fish for food.
[27]*get a new man*] Caliban bids Prospero find a new servant.

ACT III.

SCENE I. *Before* PROSPERO'S *Cell.*

Enter FERDINAND, *bearing a log.*

FER.   There be some sports are painful, and their labour
      Delight in them sets off:[1] some kinds of baseness
      Are nobly undergone, and most poor matters
      Point to rich ends. This my mean task
      Would be as heavy to me as odious, but
      The mistress which I serve quickens what 's dead,
      And makes my labours pleasures: O, she is
      Ten times more gentle than her father 's crabbed,
      And he 's composed of harshness. I must remove
      Some thousands of these logs, and pile them up,
      Upon a sore injunction:[2] my sweet mistress   .
      Weeps when she sees me work, and says, such baseness
      Had never like executor. I forget:
      But these sweet thoughts do even refresh my labours,
      Most busy lest, when I do it.[3]

Enter MIRANDA; *and* PROSPERO *at a distance, unseen.*

MIR.   Alas, now, pray you,
      Work not so hard: I would the lightning had
      Burnt up those logs that you are enjoin'd to pile!
      Pray, set it down, and rest you: when this burns,

---

[1]*There be . . . sets off*] Some sports require labour, and delight in the sport is a set-off against the labour required.

[2]*Upon a sore injunction*] under pain of a severe penalty.

[3]*Most busy lest,* [or *least*] *when I do it*] may mean "least busy, least conscious of labour, when I am working my hardest." Ferdinand's preoccupation with his sweet thoughts robs the hardest work of pain, which is inversely proportioned to the severity of the labour.

'T will weep for having wearied you.[4] My father
Is hard at study; pray, now, rest yourself;
He 's safe for these three hours.

FER.   O most dear mistress,
The sun will set before I shall discharge
What I must strive to do.

MIR.   If you 'll sit down,
I 'll bear your logs the while: pray, give me that;
I 'll carry it to the pile.

FER.   No, precious creature;
I had rather crack my sinews, break my back,
Than you should such dishonour undergo,
While I sit lazy by.

MIR.   It would become me
As well as it does you: and I should do it
With much more ease; for my good will is to it,
And yours it is against.

PROS.   Poor worm, thou art infected!
This visitation shows it.

MIR.   You look wearily.

FER.   No, noble mistress; 't is fresh morning with me
When you are by at night. I do beseech you,—
Chiefly that I might set it in my prayers,—
What is your name?

MIR.   Miranda.—O my father,
I have broke your hest to say so!

FER.   Admired Miranda!
Indeed the top of admiration! worth
What 's dearest to the world! Full many a lady
I have eyed with best regard, and many a time
The harmony of their tongues hath into bondage
Brought my too diligent ear: for several virtues
Have I liked several women; never any
With so full soul, but some defect in her
Did quarrel with the noblest grace she owed,
And put it to the foil:[5] but you, O you,
So perfect and so peerless, are created
Of every creature's best!

MIR.   I do not know
One of my sex; no woman's face remember,

---

[4]'T will weep . . . you] a reference to the resinous gum which the wood exudes on being
 set alight.
[5]put it . . . foil] frustrate it; "to foil a sword-thrust" is to turn it aside, make it go astray.

Save, from my glass, mine own; nor have I seen
More that I may call men than you, good friend,
And my dear father: how features are abroad,
I am skilless of; but, by my modesty,
The jewel in my dower, I would not wish
Any companion in the world but you;
Nor can imagination form a shape,
Besides yourself, to like of. But I prattle
Something too wildly, and my father's precepts
I therein do forget.

FER.   I am, in my condition,
A prince, Miranda; I do think, a king;
I would, not so!—and would no more endure
This wooden slavery than to suffer
The flesh-fly blow my mouth. Hear my soul speak:
The very instant that I saw you, did
My heart fly[6] to your service; there resides,
To make me slave to it; and for your sake
Am I this patient log-man.

MIR.   Do you love me?

FER.   O heaven, O earth, bear witness to this sound,
And crown what I profess with kind event,[7]
If I speak true! if hollowly, invert
What best is boded me to mischief! I,
Beyond all limit of what else[8] i' the world,
Do love, prize, honour you.

MIR.   I am a fool
To weep at what I am glad of.

PROS.   Fair encounter
Of two most rare affections! Heavens rain grace
On that which breeds between 'em!

FER.   Wherefore weep you?

MIR.   At mine unworthiness, that dare not offer
What I desire to give; and much less take
What I shall die to want.[9] But this is trifling;
And all the more it seeks to hide itself,
The bigger bulk it shows. Hence, bashful cunning!
And prompt me, plain and holy innocence!

---

[6]*The flesh-fly*] The flesh-eating fly, which putrefies.
[7]*kind event*] favourable result.
[8]*what else*] whatsoever else.
[9]*to want*] by wanting.

I am your wife, if you will marry me;
If not, I 'll die your maid: to be your fellow[10]
You may deny me; but I 'll be your servant,
Whether you will or no.

FER.   My mistress, dearest;
And I thus humble ever.

MIR.   My husband, then?

FER.   Ay, with a heart as willing
As bondage e'er of freedom:[11] here 's my hand.

MIR.   And mine, with my heart in 't: and now farewell
Till half an hour hence.

FER.   A thousand thousand![12]

                          [*Exeunt* FER. *and* MIR. *severally.*

PROS.   So glad of this as they I cannot be,
Who are surprised withal; but my rejoicing
At nothing can be more. I 'll to my book;
For yet, ere supper-time, must I perform
Much business appertaining.   [*Exit.*

SCENE II. *Another Part of the Island.*

Enter CALIBAN, STEPHANO, *and* TRINCULO.

STE.   Tell not me;—when the butt is out, we will drink water; not a
drop before: therefore bear up, and board 'em.[1] Servant-monster,
drink to me.

TRIN.   Servant-monster! the folly of this island! They say there 's but
five upon this isle: we are three of them; if th' other two be brained
like us, the state totters.

STE.   Drink, servant-monster, when I bid thee: thy eyes are almost set[2]
in thy head.

TRIN.   Where should they be set else? he were a brave monster indeed, if they were set in his tail.

STE.   My man-monster hath drowned his tongue in sack: for my part,
the sea cannot drown me; I swam, ere I could recover the shore,

---

[10]*maid . . . fellow*] maidservant . . . companion of equal rank.
[11]*As bondage . . . freedom*] As ever bondman was willing to accept freedom.
[12]*A thousand thousand*] . . . farewells.

---

[1]*bear up, and board 'em*] nautical expressions: "put the helm up; go after them and
board them." Stephano means: "let us have another go at the bottle."
[2]*set*] fixed, as in a drunken stare.

five and thirty leagues off and on. By this light, thou shalt be my lieutenant, monster, or my standard.[3]

TRIN.   Your lieutenant, if you list; he 's no standard.

STE.   We 'll not run, Monsieur Monster.

TRIN.   Nor go[4] neither; but you 'll lie, like dogs, and yet say nothing neither.

STE.   Moon-calf, speak once in thy life, if thou beest a good moon-calf.

CAL.   How does thy honour? Let me lick thy shoe.
    I 'll not serve him, he is not valiant.

TRIN.   Thou liest, most ignorant monster: I am in case to justle[5] a constable. Why, thou deboshed[6] fish, thou, was there ever man a coward that hath drunk so much sack as I to-day? Wilt thou tell a monstrous lie, being but half a fish and half a monster?

CAL.   Lo, how he mocks me! wilt thou let him, my lord?

TRIN.   "Lord," quoth he! That a monster should be such a natural!

CAL.   Lo, lo, again! bite him to death, I prithee.

STE.   Trinculo, keep a good tongue in your head: if you prove a mutineer,—the next tree! The poor monster 's my subject, and he shall not suffer indignity.

CAL.   I thank my noble lord. Wilt thou be pleased to hearken once again to the suit I made to thee?

STE.   Marry, will I: kneel and repeat it; I will stand, and so shall Trinculo.

Enter ARIEL, *invisible*.

CAL.   As I told thee before, I am subject to a tyrant, a sorcerer, that by his cunning hath cheated me of the island.

ARI.   Thou liest.

CAL.   Thou liest, thou jesting monkey, thou:
    I would my valiant master would destroy thee!
    I do not lie.

STE.   Trinculo, if you trouble him any more in 's tale, by this hand, I will supplant some of your teeth.

TRIN.   Why, I said nothing.

STE.   Mum, then, and no more. Proceed.

CAL.   I say, by sorcery he got this isle;
    From me he got it. If thy greatness will

---

[3]*standard*] standard bearer. In the next line "standard" is quibblingly used for a thing which stands without support, which Caliban in his drunken condition could not.
[4]*go*] walk.
[5]*in case to justle*] just ready for hustling.
[6]*deboshed*] Shakespeare's invariable spelling of "debauched."

Revenge it on him,—for I know thou darest,
But this thing dare not,—
STE. That 's most certain.
CAL. Thou shalt be lord of it, and I 'll serve thee.
STE. How now shall this be compassed? Canst thou bring me to the
party?
CAL. Yea, yea, my lord: I 'll yield him thee asleep,
Where thou mayst knock a nail into his head.
ARI. Thou liest; thou canst not.
CAL. What a pied ninny 's[7] this! Thou scurvy patch![8]
I do beseech thy greatness, give him blows,
And take his bottle from him: when that 's gone,
He shall drink nought but brine; for I 'll not show him
Where the quick freshes[9] are.
STE. Trinculo, run into no further danger: interrupt the monster one
word further, and, by this hand, I 'll turn my mercy out o' doors,
and make a stock-fish of thee.[10]
TRIN. Why, what did I? I did nothing. I 'll go farther off.
STE. Didst thou not say he lied?
ARI. Thou liest.
STE. Do I so? take thou that. [Beats him.] As you like this, give me the
lie another time.
TRIN. I did not give the lie. Out o' your wits, and hearing too? A pox
o' your bottle! this can sack and drinking do. A murrain on your
monster, and the devil take your fingers!
CAL. Ha, ha, ha!
STE. Now, forward with your tale.—Prithee, stand farther off.
CAL. Beat him enough: after a little time,
I 'll beat him too.
STE. Stand farther.—Come, proceed.
CAL. Why, as I told thee, 't is a custom with him
I' th' afternoon to sleep: there thou mayst brain him,
Having first seized his books; or with a log
Batter his skull, or paunch him with a stake,[11]
Or cut his wezand[12] with thy knife. Remember
First to possess his books; for without them

---

[7]*pied ninny*] fool in variegated dress. Trinculo, as the king's jester, wears motley.
[8]*patch*] simpleton.
[9]*quick freshes*] springs of fresh water.
[10]*make a stock-fish of thee*] treat thee like dried cod which was well beaten before it was
cooked.
[11]*paunch . . . stake*] put a stake through his paunch, impale him on a stake.
[12]*wezand*] windpipe.

He 's but a sot,[13] as I am, nor hath not
One spirit to command: they all do hate him
As rootedly as I. Burn but his books.
He has brave utensils,[14]—for so he calls them,—
Which, when he has a house, he 'll deck withal.
And that most deeply to consider is
The beauty of his daughter; he himself
Calls her a nonpareil: I never saw a woman,
But only Sycorax my dam and she;
But she as far surpasseth Sycorax
As great'st does least.

STE.   Is it so brave a lass?

CAL.   Ay, lord; she will become thy bed, I warrant,
And bring thee forth brave brood.

STE.   Monster, I will kill this man: his daughter and I will be king and
queen,—save our Graces!—and Trinculo and thyself shall be
viceroys. Dost thou like the plot, Trinculo?

TRIN.   Excellent.

STE.   Give me thy hand: I am sorry I beat thee; but, while thou livest,
keep a good tongue in thy head.

CAL.   Within this half hour will he be asleep:
Wilt thou destroy him then?

STE.   Ay, on mine honour.

ARI.   This will I tell my master.

CAL.   Thou makest me merry; I am full of pleasure:
Let us be jocund: will you troll[15] the catch
You taught me but while-ere?[16]

STE.   At thy request, monster, I will do reason, any reason.—Come
on, Trinculo, let us sing.   [*Sings.*

          Flout 'em and scout 'em, and scout 'em and flout 'em;
                    Thought is free.[17]

CAL.   That 's not the tune.

                    [ARIEL *plays the tune on a tabor and pipe.*

STE.   What is this same?

TRIN.   This is the tune of our catch, played by the picture of Nobody.[18]

---

[13]*sot*] used in the French sense of "fool," without any notion of drunkenness.
[14]*utensils*] The accents here are on the first and third syllables.
[15]*troll*] sing glibly.
[16]*while-ere*] no uncommon form of the more familiar "ere-while," *i.e.*, a short time since.
[17]*Thought is free*] A proverbial expression.
[18]*played by the picture of Nobody*] The picture of Nobody was a common sign for trades-
    men's shops. A head was represented with legs and arms without any body. The shop of
    the Elizabethan stationer John Trundle in the Barbican was "at the signe of Nobody."

STE.   If thou beest a man, show thyself in thy likeness: if thou beest a
    devil, take 't as thou list.

TRIN.   O, forgive me my sins!

STE.   He that dies pays all debts: I defy thee. Mercy upon us!

CAL.   Art thou afeard?

STE.   No, monster, not I.

CAL.   Be not afeard; the isle is full of noises,
    Sounds and sweet airs, that give delight, and hurt not.
    Sometimes a thousand twangling instruments
    Will hum about mine ears; and sometimes voices,
    That, if I then had waked after long sleep,
    Will make me sleep again: and then, in dreaming,
    The clouds methought would open, and show riches
    Ready to drop upon me; that, when I waked,
    I cried to dream again.

STE.   This will prove a brave kingdom to me, where I shall have my
    music for nothing.

CAL.   When Prospero is destroyed.

STE.   That shall be by and by: I remember the story.

TRIN.   The sound is going away; let 's follow it, and after do our work.

STE.   Lead, monster; we 'll follow. I would I could see this taborer;[19]
    he lays it on.

TRIN.   Wilt come? I 'll follow, Stephano.   [*Exeunt.*

SCENE III. *Another Part of the Island.*

Enter ALONSO, SEBASTIAN, ANTONIO, GONZALO, ADRIAN, FRANCISCO,
and others.

GON.   By 'r lakin,[1] I can go no further, sir;
    My old bones ache: here 's a maze trod, indeed,
    Through forth-rights and meanders![2] By your patience,
    I needs must rest me.

ALON.   Old lord, I cannot blame thee,
    Who am myself attach'd[3] with weariness,
    To the dulling of my spirits: sit down, and rest.
    Even here I will put off my hope, and keep it

---

[19]*this taborer*] this drummer. Ariel, according to the stage direction, has been playing
on a tabor (*i.e.*, a drum worn at the side) and a pipe.

---

[1]*By 'r lakin*] By our lady, by the Virgin Mary.
[2]*forth-rights and meanders*] straight and winding paths.
[3]*attach'd*] seized; used figuratively in its legal significance.

No longer for my flatterer: he is drown'd
Whom thus we stray to find; and the sea mocks
Our frustrate search on land. Well, let him go.

ANT.   [*Aside to* SEB.] I am right glad that he 's so out of hope.
Do not, for one repulse, forgo the purpose
That you resolved to effect.

SEB.   [*Aside to* ANT.] The next advantage
Will we take throughly.

ANT.   [*Aside to* SEB.] Let it be to-night;
For, now they are oppress'd with travel, they
Will not, nor cannot, use such vigilance
As when they are fresh.

SEB.   [*Aside to* ANT.] I say, to-night: no more.

                                [*Solemn and strange music.*

ALON.   What harmony is this?—My good friends, hark!
GON.   Marvellous sweet music!

Enter PROSPERO *above, invisible. Enter several strange Shapes, bring-
ing in a banquet: they dance about it with gentle actions of salu-
tation; and, inviting the King, &c. to eat, they depart.*

ALON.   Give us kind keepers, heavens!—What were these?
SEB.   A living drollery.[4] Now I will believe
That there are unicorns; that in Arabia
There is one tree, the phœnix' throne; one phœnix[5]
At this hour reigning there.

ANT.   I 'll believe both;
And what does else want credit, come to me,
And I 'll be sworn 't is true: travellers ne'er did lie,
Though fools at home condemn 'em.

GON.   If in Naples
I should report this now, would they believe me?
If I should say, I saw such islanders,—
For, certes, these are people of the island,—
Who, though they are of monstrous shape, yet, note,
Their manners are more gentle-kind than of
Our human generation you shall find
Many, nay, almost any.

PROS.   [*Aside.*] Honest lord,
Thou hast said well; for some of you there present

---

[4]*A living drollery*] A puppet show presented by living persons.
[5]*one phœnix*] Here Shakespeare seems to have had in mind the passage in Lyly's
Euphues: "For as there is but *one Phœnix* in the world, so there is but *one tree in Arabia*
wherein she buyldeth." The faith in the myth was widespread.

    Are worse than devils.
ALON.   I cannot too much muse
    Such shapes, such gesture, and such sound, expressing—
    Although they want the use of tongue—a kind
    Of excellent dumb discourse.
PROS.   [*Aside.*] Praise in departing.[6]
FRAN. They vanish'd strangely.
SEB.   No matter, since
    They have left their viands behind; for we have stomachs.—
    Will 't please you taste of what is here?
ALON.   Not I.
GON.   Faith, sir, you need not fear. Where we were boys,
    Who would believe that there were mountaineers
    Dew-lapp'd like bulls,[7] whose throats had hanging at 'em
    Wallets of flesh? or that there were such men
    Whose heads stood in their breasts?[8] which now we find
    Each putter-out of five for one[9] will bring us
    Good warrant of.
ALON.   I will stand to, and feed,
    Although my last: no matter, since I feel
    The best is past. Brother, my lord the duke,
    Stand to, and do as we.

Thunder and lightning. Enter ARIEL, *like a harpy; claps his wings upon
    the table; and, with a quaint device, the banquet vanishes.*

ARI.   You are three men of sin, whom Destiny,—
    That hath to instrument[10] this lower world
    And what is in 't,—the never-surfeited sea
    Hath caused to belch up you; and on this island,
    Where man doth not inhabit,—you 'mongst men

---

[6]*Praise in departing*] A proverbial phrase: "reserve your praise for your departure," "wait
to see how it turns out."

[7]*Dew-lapp'd like bulls*] With pendulous skin at the throat, as in the case of bulls; a reference to sufferers from goitre, to which the inhabitants of mountainous districts are
liable.

[8]*men Whose heads . . . breasts*] Ralegh in his *Discovery of Guiana* (1595) reported that
west of the Oronoko River was a nation of people "whose heads appeare not above
their shoulders . . . they are reported to have their eyes in their shoulders and their
mouths in the middle of their breasts."

[9]*putter-out of five for one*] Merchants were in the habit of accepting from those who em-
barked on long and venturesome voyages a sum of money, on the understanding that
it should become their property if the vessel failed to return home, but should be re-
stored fivefold if the ship came safely to port. The voyager thus wagered five to one on
his chance of surviving the dangers of the voyage.

[10]*to instrument*] for instrument.

Being most unfit to live. I have made you mad;
And even with such-like valour men hang and drown
Their proper selves.   [ALON., SEB. *&c. draw their swords.*
                        You fools! I and my fellows
Are ministers of Fate: the elements,
Of whom your swords are temper'd, may as well
Wound the loud winds, or with bemock'd-at stabs
Kill the still-closing waters, as diminish
One dowle[11] that 's in my plume: my fellow-ministers
Are like invulnerable. If you could hurt,
Your swords are now too massy for your strengths,
And will not be uplifted. But remember,—
For that 's my business to you,—that you three
From Milan did supplant good Prospero;
Exposed unto the sea, which hath requit it,
Him and his innocent child: for which foul deed
The powers, delaying, not forgetting, have
Incensed the seas and shores, yea, all the creatures,
Against your peace. Thee of thy son, Alonso,
They have bereft; and do pronounce by me:
Lingering perdition—worse than any death
Can be at once—shall step by step attend
You and your ways; whose wraths to guard you from,—
Which here, in this most desolate isle, else falls
Upon your heads,—is nothing but heart-sorrow
And a clear life ensuing.[12]

He vanishes in thunder; then, to soft music, enter the Shapes again,
    and dance, with mocks and mows, and carrying out the table.

PROS.   Bravely the figure[13] of this harpy hast thou
    Perform'd, my Ariel; a grace it had, devouring:
    Of my instruction hast thou nothing bated
    In what thou hadst to say: so, with good life
    And observation strange,[14] my meaner ministers
    Their several kinds have done. My high charms work,
    And these mine enemies are all knit up

---

[11]*dowle*] a particle of down; the word is still used in provincial English dialects. It is
sometimes spelt "dowlne."
[12]*whose wraths . . . ensuing*] The subject of the relative "whose" is "the seas and shores"
and "all the creatures." The meaning is that delivery from their wraths can only come
from heartfelt repentance and amended life hereafter.
[13]*figure*] role, assumed part.
[14]*with good life . . . strange*] with presentation of their characters to the life, and rare at-
tention to their several roles.

                    In their distractions: they now are in my power;
                    And in these fits I leave them, while I visit
                    Young Ferdinand,—whom they suppose is drown'd,—
                    And his and mine loved darling.   [*Exit above.*

GON.   I' the name of something holy, sir, why stand you
                    In this strange stare?

ALON.   O, it is monstrous, monstrous!
                    Methought the billows spoke, and told me of it;[15]
                    The winds did sing it to me; and the thunder,
                    That deep and dreadful organ-pipe, pronounced
                    The name of Prosper: it did bass[16] my trespass.
                    Therefore my son i' th' ooze is bedded; and
                    I 'll seek him deeper than e'er plummet sounded,
                    And with him there lie mudded.   [*Exit.*

SEB.   But one fiend at a time,
                    I 'll fight their legions o'er.

ANT.   I 'll be thy second.

                              [*Exeunt* SEB. *and* ANT.

GON.   All three of them are desperate: their great guilt,
                    Like poison given to work a great time after,[17]
                    Now 'gins to bite the spirits. I do beseech you,
                    That are of suppler joints, follow them swiftly,
                    And hinder them from what this ecstasy[18]
                    May now provoke them to.

ADR.   Follow, I pray you.   [*Exeunt.*

---

[15]*of it*] of my sin; "my traspass" (*see three lines after*).

[16]*bass*] that is, the thunder proclaimed my sin in bass notes.

[17]*Like poison . . . after*] It was believed that poisons could be so tempered as to operate
a long time after their administration.

[18]*ecstasy*] fit of madness, frenzy.

ACT IV.

SCENE I. *Before* PROSPERO's *Cell*.

Enter PROSPERO, FERDINAND, *and* MIRANDA.

PROS.   If I have too austerely punish'd you,
    Your compensation makes amends; for I
    Have given you here a third[1] of mine own life,
    Or that for which I live; who once again
    I tender to thy hand: all thy vexations
    Were but my trials of thy love, and thou
    Hast strangely[2] stood the test: here, afore Heaven,
    I ratify this my rich gift. O Ferdinand,
    Do not smile at me that I boast her off,[3]
    For thou shalt find she will outstrip all praise,
    And make it halt behind her
FER.   I do believe it
    Against an oracle.
PROS.   Then, as my gift, and thine own acquisition
    Worthily purchased, take my daughter: but
    If thou dost break her virgin-knot before
    All sanctimonious[4] ceremonies may
    With full and holy rite be minister'd,
    No sweet aspersion[5] shall the heavens let fall
    To make this contrast grow; but barren hate,

---

[1] *a third*] The reading is not quite clear. It may well be that he regards his life as made up of three parts—himself, his realm, and his daughter. He declares at the end of the play that every *third* thought shall be his grave, a statement that confirms the triplicity of his interests.

[2] *strangely*] wonderfully.

[3] *boast her off*] "off" is often used adverbially as an intensitive, meaning "to the best advantage." Cf. the common phrase "come *off*," [*i.e.*, turn out well].

[4] *sanctimonious*] sacred, without the ironical intention, which often attached to it in Shakespeare's day, and invariably attaches to it now.

[5] *aspersion*] in the Latin sense of "sprinkling."

48

Sour-eyed disdain and discord shall bestrew
The union of your bed with weeds so loathly
That you shall hate it both: therefore take heed,
As Hymen's lamps shall light you.[6]

FER.   As I hope
For quiet days, fair issue and long life,
With such love as 't is now, the murkiest den,
The most opportune place, the strong'st suggestion
Our worser Genius can,[7] shall never melt
Mine honour into lust, to take away
The edge of that day's celebration
When I shall think, or Phœbus' steeds are founder'd,[8]
Or Night kept chain'd below.

PROS.   Fairly spoke.
Sit, then, and talk with her; she is thine own.
What, Ariel! my industrious servant, Ariel!

Enter ARIEL.

ARI.   What would my potent master? here I am.
PROS.   Thou and thy meaner fellows your last service
Did worthily perform; and I must use you
In such another trick. Go bring the rabble,[9]
O'er whom I give thee power, here to this place:
Incite them to quick motion; for I must
Bestow upon the eyes of this young couple
Some vanity[10] of mine art: it is my promise,
And they expect it from me.

ARI.   Presently?
PROS.   Ay, with a twink.[11]
ARI.   Before you can say, "come," and "go,"
And breathe twice, and cry, "so, so,"
Each one, tripping on his toe,
Will be here with mop and mow.[12]
Do you love me, master? no?

[6]*As Hymen's lamps . . . you*] According as Hymen's lamps shall guide you. Only follow the light of Hymen's lamps.

[7]*the strong'st suggestion . . . can*] the strongest temptation of which our worser genius is capable.

[8]*Phœbus' steeds are founder'd*] the general meaning is that the sun is at a standstill. "Foundering" was a recognised disease in horses, which rendered all movement impossible.

[9]*rabble*] the crew of meaner spirits.

[10]*Some vanity*] Some illusion.

[11]*with a twink*] in a twinkling.

[12]*with mop and mow*] with gibbering grimace.

PROS.   Dearly, my delicate Ariel. Do not approach
    Till thou dost hear me call.
ARI.   Well, I conceive.   [*Exit.*
PROS.   Look thou be true; do not give dalliance
    Too much the rein: the strongest oaths are straw
    To the fire i' the blood: be more abstemious,
    Or else, good night your vow!
FER.   I warrant you, sir;
    The white cold virgin snow upon my heart
    Abates the ardour of my liver.
PROS.   Well.
    Now come, my Ariel! bring a corollary,[13]
    Rather than want a spirit: appear, and pertly!
    No tongue! all eyes! be silent.   [*Soft music.*

Enter IRIS.

IRIS.   Ceres, most bounteous lady, thy rich leas
    Of wheat, rye, barley, vetches, oats, and pease;
    Thy turfy mountains, where live nibbling sheep,
    And flat meads thatch'd with stover,[14] them to keep;
    Thy banks with pioned and twilled[15] brims,
    Which spongy April at thy hest betrims,
    To make cold nymphs chaste crowns;[16] and thy broom-groves,[17]
    Whose shadow the dismissed bachelor loves,
    Being lass-lorn; thy pole-clipt[18] vineyard;
    And thy sea-marge, sterile and rocky-hard,
    Where thou thyself dost air;—the queen o' the sky,
    Whose watery arch and messenger am I,
    Bids thee leave these; and with her sovereign grace,
    Here on this grass-plot, in this very place,
    To come and sport:—her peacocks fly amain:
    Approach, rich Ceres, her to entertain.

Enter CERES.

---

[13]*a corollary*] a surplus, more than is sufficient.
[14]*stover*] coarse grass used for thatching.
[15]*pioned and twilled*] The meaning is obscure. The line seems to describe the river-banks in winter or early spring before flowers adorn them, and when their brims or edges have been "pioned" (dug out?) and "twilled" (hoed into ridges?).
[16]*chaste crowns*] a common meadow plant with white flowers, which blossoms in "spongy [*i.e.*, rainy] April."
[17]*broom-groves*] a species of broom that grows to a considerable height.
[18]*pole-clipt*] embraced or fenced about by poles.

CER.   Hail, many-colour'd messenger, that ne er
        Dost disobey the wife of Jupiter;
        Who, with thy saffron wings, upon my flowers
        Diffusest honey-drops, refreshing showers;
        And with each end of thy blue bow dust crown
        My bosky acres and my unshrubb'd down,[19]
        Rich scarf to my proud earth;—why hath thy queen
        Summon'd me hither, to this short-grass'd green?

IRIS.   A contract of true love to celebrate;
        And some donation freely to estate[20]
        On the blest lovers.

CER.   Tell me, heavenly bow,
        If Venus or her son, as thou dost know,
        Do now attend the queen? Since they did plot
        The means that dusky Dis[21] my daughter got,
        Her and her blind boy's scandal'd[22] company
        I have forsworn.

IRIS.   Of her society
        Be not afraid: I met her Deity
        Cutting the clouds towards Paphos, and her son
        Dove-drawn with her. Here thought they to have done
        Some wanton charm upon this man and maid,
        Whose vows are, that no bed-right shall be paid
        Till Hymen's torch be lighted: but in vain;
        Mars's hot minion is returned again;
        Her waspish-headed son has broke his arrows,
        Swears he will shoot no more, but play with sparrows,
        And be a boy right out.

CER.   High'st queen of state,
        Great Juno, comes; I know her by her gait.

Enter JUNO.

JUNO.   How does my bounteous sister? Go with me
        To bless this twain, that they may prosperous be,
        And honour'd in their issue.   [*They sing*:

JUNO.   Honour, riches, marriage-blessing,
                Long continuance, and increasing,
                Hourly joys be still upon you!
                Juno sings her blessings on you.

---

[19]*My bosky . . . down*] My wooded acres and bare downs.
[20]*to estate*] to settle.
[21]*dusky Dis*] The reference is to Pluto's rape of Proserpina, of which the story is told in
   Ovid's *Metamorphoses*.
[22]*scandal'd*] scandalous, disgraceful.

CER.   Earth's increase, foison plenty,[23]
                           Barns and garners never empty;
                           Vines with clustering bunches growing;
                           Plants with goodly burthen bowing;
                           Spring come to you at the farthest[24]
                           In the very end of harvest!
                           Scarcity and want shall shun you;
                           Ceres' blessing so is on you.

FER.   This is a most majestic vision, and
       Harmonious charmingly.[25] May I be bold
       To think these spirits?
PROS.   Spirits, which by mine art
       I have from their confines call'd to enact
       My present fancies.
FER.   Let me live here ever;
       So rare a wonder'd father[26] and a wise
       Makes this place Paradise.

              [JUNO *and* CERES *whisper, and send* IRIS *on employment.*
PROS.   Sweet, now, silence!
       Juno and Ceres whisper seriously;
       There 's something else to do: hush, and be mute,
       Or else our spell is marr'd.

IRIS.   You nymphs, call'd Naiads, of the windring[27] brooks,
        With your sedged crowns and ever-harmless looks,
        Leave your crisp[28] channels and, on this green land
        Answer your summons; Juno does command:
        Come, temperate nymphs, and help to celebrate
        A contract of true love; be not too late.

Enter certain Nymphs.

        You sunburn'd sicklemen, of August weary,
        Come hither from the furrow, and be merry:
        Make holiday; your rye-straw hats put on,
        And these fresh nymphs encounter every one
        In country footing.[29]

---

[23]*foison plenty*] harvest in abundance.
[24]*at the farthest*] at the latest, when the harvest is over.
[25]*charmingly*] in magical fashion.
[26]*So rare a wonder'd father*] a father able to perform such rare wonders.
[27]*windring*] apparently "winding."
[28]*crisp*] with the water curled or rippled by the breeze.
[29]*footing*] dance.

*Enter certain Reapers, properly habited: they join with the Nymphs in
    a graceful dance; towards the end whereof* PROSPERO *starts sud-
    denly, and speaks; after which, to a strange, hollow, and confused
    noise, they heavily vanish.*

PROS.   [*Aside.*] I had forgot that foul conspiracy
    Of the beast Caliban and his confederates
    Against my life: the minute of their plot
    Is almost come. [*To the Spirits.*] Well done! avoid;[30] no more!
FER.   This is strange: your father's in some passion
    That works him strongly.
MIR.   Never till this day
    Saw I him touch'd with anger so distemper'd.
PROS.   You do look, my son, in a moved sort,[31]
    As if you were dismay'd: be cheerful, sir.
    Our revels now are ended. These our actors,
    As I foretold you, were all spirits, and
    Are melted into air, into thin air:
    And, like the baseless fabric of this vision,
    The cloud-capp'd towers, the gorgeous palaces,
    The solemn temples, the great globe itself,
    Yea, all which it inherit,[32] shall dissolve,
    And, like this insubstantial pageant faded,
    Leave not a rack[33] behind. We are such stuff
    As dreams are made on; and our little life
    Is rounded with a sleep. Sir, I am vex'd;
    Bear with my weakness; my old brain is troubled:
    Be not disturb'd with my infirmity:
    If you be pleased, retire into my cell,
    And there repose: a turn or two I'll walk,
    To still my beating mind.
FER. MIR.   We wish your peace.   [*Exeunt.*
PROS.   Come with a thought.[34] I thank thee, Ariel: come.

Enter ARIEL.

ARI.   Thy thoughts I cleave to. What's thy pleasure?
PROS.   Spirit,
    We must prepare to meet with[35] Caliban.

[30]*avoid*] begone.
[31]*in a moved sort*] in a troubled state.
[32]*all which it inherit*] all the things which possess or occupy the globe.
[33]*a rack*] a wreath of cloud, a bank of light cloud.
[34]*with a thought*] quick as thought.
[35]*meet with*] encounter, counteract.

ARI.   Ay, my commander: when I presented[36] Ceres,
    I thought to have told thee of it; but I fear'd
    Lest I might anger thee.
PROS.   Say again, where didst thou leave these varlets?
ARI.   I told you, sir, they were red-hot with drinking;
    So full of valour that they smote the air
    For breathing in their faces; beat the ground
    For kissing of their feet; yet always bending
    Towards their project. Then I beat my tabor;
    At which, like unback'd colts,[37] they prick'd their ears,
    Advanced[38] their eyelids, lifted up their noses
    As they smelt music: so I charm'd their ears,
    That, calf-like, they my lowing follow'd through
    Tooth'd briers, sharp furzes, pricking goss,[39] and thorns,
    Which enter'd their frail shins: at last I left them
    I' the filthy-mantled pool beyond your cell,
    There dancing up to the chins, that the foul lake
    O'erstunk their feet.
PROS.   This was well done, my bird.
    Thy shape invisible retain thou still:
    The trumpery in my house, go bring it hither,
    For stale[40] to catch these thieves.
ARI.   I go, I go.   [*Exit.*
PROS.   A devil, a born devil, on whose nature
    Nurture can never stick;[41] on whom my pains,
    Humanely taken, all, all lost, quite lost;
    And as with age his body uglier grows,
    So his mind cankers. I will plague them all,
    Even to roaring.

Re-enter ARIEL, *loaden with glistering apparel, &c.*

        Come, hang them on this line.[42]

PROSPERO *and* ARIEL *remain, invisible. Enter* CALIBAN, STEPHANO,
    and TRINCULO, *all wet.*

---

[36]*presented*] presented the part of.
[37]*unback'd colts*] colts that never have been ridden.
[38]*Advanced*] Raised.
[39]*goss*] gorse.
[40]*The trumpery . . . stale*] The gaudy apparel, which is to be used as "stale," *i.e.*, decoy
  or lure.
[41]*Nurture . . . stick*] Education or training can never adhere to.
[42]*line*] line tree or linden. Later, Stephano addresses the tree as "mistress *line*," and
  puns on the word [*see footnote 47*].

CAL. Pray you, tread softly, that the blind mole may not
      Hear a foot fall: we now are near his cell.
STE. Monster, your fairy, which you say is a harmless fairy, has done
      little better than played the Jack[43] with us.
TRIN. Monster, I do smell all horse-piss; at which my nose is in great
      indignation.
STE. So is mine. Do you hear, monster? If I should take a displeasure
      against you, look you,—
TRIN. Thou wert but a lost monster.
CAL. Good my lord, give me thy favour still.
      Be patient, for the prize I 'll bring thee to
      Shall hoodwink[44] this mischance: therefore speak softly.
      All 's hush'd as midnight yet.
TRIN. Ay, but to lose our bottles in the pool,—
STE. There is not only disgrace and dishonour in that, monster, but
      an infinite loss.
TRIN. That 's more to me than my wetting: yet this is your harmless
      fairy, monster.
STE. I will fetch off my bottle, though I be o'er ears for my labour.
CAL. Prithee, my king, be quiet. See'st thou here,
      This is the mouth o' the cell: no noise, and enter.
      Do that good mischief which may make this island
      Thine own for ever, and I, thy Caliban,
      For aye thy foot-licker.
STE. Give me thy hand. I do begin to have bloody thoughts.
TRIN. O King Stephano! O peer! O worthy Stephano! look what a
      wardrobe[45] here is for thee!
CAL. Let it alone, thou fool; it is but trash.
TRIN. O, ho, monster! we know what belongs to a frippery.[46] O King
      Stephano!
STE. Put off that gown, Trinculo; by this hand I 'll have that gown.
TRIN. Thy Grace shall have it.
CAL. The dropsy drown this fool! what do you mean
      To dote thus on such luggage? Let 's alone,
      And do the murder first: if he awake,
      From toe to crown he 'll fill our skins with pinches,
      Make us strange stuff.

---

[43]*played the Jack*] played the fool or knave.
[44]*hoodwink*] put out of sight.
[45]*O King Stephano . . . wardrobe*] An allusion to the old popular ballad called *Take thy Old Cloak about Thee*, of which a stanza concerning King Stephen's scanty wardrobe begins, "King Stephen was a worthy peer, His breeches cost him but a crown."
[46]*frippery*] old clothes shop.

STE. Be you quiet, monster. Mistress line,[47] is not this my jerkin?
   Now is the jerkin under the line: now, jerkin, you are like to lose
   your hair, and prove a bald jerkin.

TRIN. Do, do: we steal by line and level,[48] an 't like your Grace.

STE. I thank thee for that jest; here 's a garment for 't: wit shall not
   go unrewarded while I am king of this country. "Steal by line
   and level" is an excellent pass of pate;[49] there 's another garment
   for 't.

TRIN. Monster, come, put some lime[50] upon your fingers, and away
   with the rest.

CAL. I will have none on 't: we shall lose our time,
   And all be turn'd to barnacles,[51] or to apes
   With foreheads villanous low.

STE. Monster, lay-to your fingers: help to bear this away where my
   hogshead of wine is, or I 'll turn you out of my kingdom: go to,
   carry this.

TRIN. And this.

STE. Ay, and this.

*A noise of hunters heard. Enter divers Spirits, in shape of dogs and
   hounds, hunting them about; PROSPERO and ARIEL setting them
   on.*

PROS. Hey, Mountain, hey!

ARI. Silver! there it goes, Silver!

PROS. Fury, Fury! there, Tyrant, there! hark, hark!
                         [CAL., STE., *and* TRIN. *are driven out.*
   Go charge my goblins that they grind their joints
   With dry convulsions;[52] shorten up their sinews
   With aged cramps; and more pinch-spotted make them
   Than pard or cat o' mountain.[53]

---

[47]*Mistress line*] Addressed to the line or linden tree, on which the clothes are hung.
   The word "line" is jestingly used for the equinoctial line, in crossing which the
   voyagers were often reported to suffer loss of hair, owing to fever or other violent
   distemper.

[48]*line and level*] according to rule; a common phrase, which continues the quibbling
   on the word "line."

[49]*pass of pate*] thrust of wit. "Pass" is a technical fencing term.

[50]*lime*] bird lime, to which things stick.

[51]*barnacles*] The shell-fish of that name were popularly reputed to develop into geese.
   The word was applied indifferently to both shell-fish and geese. Caliban uses it in the
   latter sense.

[52]*dry convulsions*] convulsions due to morbid dryness of the joints.

[53]*cat o' mountain*] A term applied by contemporary authors both to the leopard and the
   wild cat.

ARI.   Hark, they roar!
PROS.   Let them be hunted soundly. At this hour
         Lie at my mercy all mine enemies:
         Shortly shall all my labours end, and thou
         Shalt have the air at freedom: for a little
         Follow, and do me service.   [*Exeunt*.

ACT V.

SCENE I. *Before the Cell of* PROSPERO.

Enter PROSPERO *in his magic robes, and* ARIEL.

PROS.   Now does my project gather to a head:
    My charms crack not;[1] my spirits obey; and time
    Goes upright with his carriage.[2]
    How 's the day?
ARI.   On the sixth hour; at which time, my lord,
    You said our work should cease.
PROS.   I did say so,
    When first I raised the tempest.
    Say, my spirit,
    How fares the king and 's followers?
ARI.   Confined together
    In the same fashion as you gave in charge,
    Just as you left them; all prisoners, sir
    In the line-grove which weather-fends[3] your cell;
    They cannot budge till your release.[4] The king,
    His brother, and yours, abide all three distracted,
    And the remainder mourning over them,
    Brimful of sorrow and dismay; but chiefly
    Him that you term'd, sir, "The good old lord, Gonzalo";
    His tears run down his beard, like winter's drops
    From eaves of reeds. Your charm so strongly works 'em,
    That if you now beheld them, your affections
    Would become tender.

[1]*crack not*] have no flaw.
[2]*Goes upright . . . carriage*] Walks upright with what he has to carry, does not bend
under his load.
[3]*line-grove . . . weather-fends*] grove of lines or linden-trees which protects from the
weather.
[4]*your release*] release (of them) by you.

PROS.   Dost thou think so, spirit?
ARI.   Mine would, sir, were I human.
PROS.   And mine shall.
        Hast thou, which art but air, a touch, a feeling
        Of their afflictions, and shall not myself,
        One of their kind, that relish all as sharply,
        Passion as they,[5] be kindlier moved than thou art?
        Though with their high wrongs I am struck to the quick,
        Yet with my nobler reason 'gainst my fury
        Do I take part: the rarer action is
        In virtue than in vengeance: they being penitent,
        The sole drift of my purpose doth extend
        Not a frown further. Go release them, Ariel:
        My charms I 'll break, their senses I 'll restore,
        And they shall be themselves.
ARI.   I 'll fetch them, sir.   [Exit.
PROS.   Ye elves of hills, brooks, standing lakes, and groves;
        And ye that on the sands with printless foot
        Do chase the ebbing Neptune, and do fly him
        When he comes back; you demi-puppets[6] that
        By moonshine do the green sour ringlets[7] make,
        Whereof the ewe not bites; and you whose pastime
        Is to make midnight mushrooms, that rejoice
        To hear the solemn curfew; by whose aid—
        Weak masters[8] though ye be—I have bedimm'd
        The noontide sun, call'd forth the mutinous winds,
        And 'twixt the green sea and the azured vault
        Set roaring war: to the dread rattling thunder
        Have I given fire, and rifted Jove's stout oak
        With his own bolt; the strong-based promontory
        Have I made shake, and by the spurs[9] pluck'd up
        The pine and cedar: graves at my command
        Have waked their sleepers, oped, and let 'em forth
        By my so potent art. But this rough magic
        I here abjure; and, when I have required
        Some heavenly music,—which even now I do,—
        To work mine end upon their senses, that

[5]*that relish . . . as they*] who have the same quick sensibility, are moved by the same passion as they.
[6]*demi-puppets*] dwarf-puppets, tiny elves.
[7]*green sour ringlets*] ringlets of grass, commonly called "fairy rings," of which the colour
  is a deeper green than usual, and the taste is reputed to be sour.
[8]*Weak masters*] Puny controllers of magical power [*see footnote* 6: "demi-puppets"].
[9]*spurs*] the longest roots of trees.

This airy charm is for, I 'll break my staff,
Bury it certain fathoms in the earth,
And deeper than did ever plummet sound
I 'll drown my book.   [*Solemn music.*

Re-enter ARIEL *before: then* ALONSO, *with a frantic gesture, attended by*
GONZALO; SEBASTIAN *and* ANTONIO *in like manner, attended by*
ADRIAN *and* FRANCISCO: *they all enter the circle which* PROSPERO
had made, and there stand charmed; which PROSPERO *observing,*
speaks:

A solemn air, and the best comforter
To an unsettled fancy, cure thy brains,
Now useless, boil'd[10] within thy skull! There stand,
For you are spell-stopp'd.
Holy Gonzalo, honourable man,
Mine eyes, even sociable to the show of thine,[11]
Fall fellowly drops. The charm dissolves apace;
And as the morning steals upon the night,
Melting the darkness, so their rising senses
Begin to chase the ignorant fumes that mantle
Their clearer reason. O good Gonzalo,
My true preserver, and a loyal sir
To him thou follow'st! I will pay thy graces
Home both in word and deed. Most cruelly
Didst thou, Alonso, use me and my daughter:
Thy brother was a furtherer in the act.
Thou art pinch'd for 't now, Sebastian. Flesh and blood,
You, brother mine, that entertain'd ambition,
Expell'd remorse and nature;[12] who, with Sebastian,—
Whose inward pinches therefore are most strong,—
Would here have kill'd your king; I do forgive thee,
Unnatural though thou art. Their understanding
Begins to swell;[13] and the approaching tide
Will shortly fill the reasonable shore,[14]
That now lies foul and muddy. Not one of them
That yet looks on me, or would know me: Ariel,
Fetch me the hat and rapier in my cell:

[10]*boil'd*] overexcited, unbalanced.
[11]*sociable to . . . thine*] sympathetic with the feeling which thine eyes betray.
[12]*remorse and nature*] pity and natural affection.
[13]*Their understanding . . . swell*] Their consciousness (which had ebbed to the lowest point) is turning towards full tide.
[14]*reasonable shore*] shore of reason.

     I will discase me, and myself present
     As I was sometime Milan: quickly, spirit;
     Thou shalt ere long be free.

ARIEL *sings and helps to attire him.*

          [15]Where the bee sucks, there suck I:
          In a cowslip's bell I lie;
          There I couch when owls do cry.
          On the bat's back I do fly
          After summer[16] merrily.
        Merrily, merrily shall I live now
        Under the blossom that hangs on the bough.

PROS.   Why, that 's my dainty Ariel! I shall miss thee;
     But yet thou shalt have freedom: so, so, so.
     To the king's ship, invisible as thou art:
     There shalt thou find the mariners asleep
     Under the hatches; the master and the boatswain
     Being awake, enforce them to this place,
     And presently, I prithee.
ARI.   I drink the air before me, and return
     Or ere your pulse twice beat.   [*Exit.*
GON.   All torment, trouble, wonder and amazement
     Inhabits here: some heavenly power guide us
     Out of this fearful country!
PROS.   Behold, sir king,
     The wronged Duke of Milan, Prospero:
     For more assurance that a living prince
     Does now speak to thee, I embrace thy body;
     And to thee and thy company I bid
     A hearty welcome.
ALON.   Whether thou be'st he or no,
     Or some enchanted trifle[17] to abuse me,
     As late I have been, I not know: thy pulse
     Beats, as of flesh and blood; and, since I saw thee,
     The affliction of my mind amends, with which,
     I fear, a madness held me: this must crave—
     An if this be at all[18]—a most strange story.
     Thy dukedom I resign, and do entreat

---

[15]*Where the bee sucks . . . hangs on the bough*] This song has been credited to R. Johnson, a well-known composer of Shakespeare's day.

[16]*After summer*] In pursuit of summer.

[17]*enchanted trifle*] trick of enchantment.

[18]*An if this be at all*] If there be reality in all this.

Thou pardon me my wrongs.—But how should Prospero
Be living and be here?
PROS.   First, noble friend,
Let me embrace thine age, whose honour cannot
Be measured or confined.
GON.   Whether this be
Or be not, I 'll not swear.
PROS.   You do yet taste
Some subtilties[19] o' the isle, that will not let you
Believe things certain. Welcome, my friends all!
    [*Aside to* SEB. *and* ANT.] But you, my brace of lords, were I so
        minded,
I here could pluck his Highness' frown upon you,
And justify[20] you traitors: at this time
I will tell no tales.
SEB.   [*Aside.*] The devil speaks in him.
PROS.   No.
For you, most wicked sir, whom to call brother
Would even infect my mouth, I do forgive
Thy rankest fault,—all of them; and require
My dukedom of thee, which perforce, I know,
Thou must restore.
ALON.   If thou be'st Prospero,
Give us particulars of thy preservation;
How thou hast met us here, who three hours since
Were wreck'd upon this shore; where I have lost—
How sharp the point of this remembrance is!—
My dear son Ferdinand.
PROS.   I am woe for 't, sir.
ALON.   Irreparable is the loss; and patience
Says it is past her cure.
PROS.   I rather think
You have not sought her help, of whose soft grace
For the like loss I have her sovereign aid,
And rest myself content.
ALON.   You the like loss!
PROS.   As great to me as late; and, supportable
To make the dear loss,[21] have I means much weaker

---

[19]*subtilties*] deceptions, or illusions. The word was specifically applied to devices in pastry and confectionery, a circumstance which explains Prospero's use of the word "taste."

[20]*justify*] prove.

[21]*As great . . . loss*] As great to me as it is recent; and, to make this bitter loss bearable, etc.

Than you may call to comfort you, for I
Have lost my daughter.
ALON.   A daughter?
O heavens, that they were living both in Naples,
The king and queen there! that they were, I wish
Myself were mudded in that oozy bed
Where my son lies. When did you lose your daughter?
PROS.   In this last tempest. I perceive, these lords
At this encounter do so much admire,
That they devour their reason, and scarce think
Their eyes do offices of truth, their words
Are natural breath:[22] but, howsoe'er you have
Been justled from your senses, know for certain
That I am Prospero, and that very duke
Which was thrust forth of Milan; who most strangely
Upon this shore, where you were wreck'd, was landed,
To be the lord on 't. No more yet of this;
For 't is a chronicle of day by day,
Not a relation for a breakfast, nor
Befitting this first meeting. Welcome, sir;
This cell 's my court: here have I few attendants,
And subjects none abroad: pray you, look in.
My dukedom since you have given me again,
I will requite you with as good a thing;
At least bring forth a wonder, to content ye
As much as me my dukedom.

Here PROSPERO *discovers* FERDINAND *and* MIRANDA *playing at chess.*

MIR.   Sweet lord, you play me false.
FER.   No, my dear'st love,
I would not for the world.
MIR.   Yes, for a score of kingdoms you should wrangle,
And I would call it fair play.[23]
ALON.   If this prove
A vision of the island, one dear son
Shall I twice lose.
SEB.   A most high miracle!
FER.   Though the seas threaten, they are merciful;
I have cursed them without cause.   [*Kneels.*

---

[22]*Are natural breath*] Come from human beings.
[23]*Yes, . . . fair play*] The meaning required is: "Should you win a stake of twenty kingdoms by cheating me at the game, I would call it fair play." "Wrangle" is employed
in the unusual sense of "compete by unworthy means."

ALON.   Now all the blessings
    Of a glad father compass thee about!
    Arise, and say how thou camest here.
MIR.   O, wonder!
    How many goodly creatures are there here!
    How beauteous mankind is! O brave new world,
    That has such people in 't!
PROS.   'T is new to thee.
ALON.   What is this maid with whom thou wast at play?
    Your eld'st acquaintance cannot be three hours:
    Is she the goddess that hath sever'd us,
    And brought us thus together?
FER.   Sir, she is mortal;
    But by immortal Providence she 's mine:
    I chose her when I could not ask my father
    For his advice, nor thought I had one. She
    Is daughter to this famous Duke of Milan,
    Of whom so often I have heard renown,
    But never saw before; of whom I have
    Received a second life; and second father
    This lady makes him to me.
ALON.   I am hers:
    But, O, how oddly will it sound that I
    Must ask my child forgiveness!
PROS.   There, sir, stop:
    Let us not burthen our remembrances with
    A heaviness that 's gone.
GON.   I have inly wept,
    Or should have spoke ere this. Look down, you gods,
    And on this couple drop a blessed crown!
    For it is you that have chalk'd forth the way
    Which brought us hither.
ALON.   I say, Amen, Gonzalo!
GON.   Was Milan thrust from Milan, that his issue
    Should become kings of Naples? O, rejoice
    Beyond a common joy! and set it down
    With gold on lasting pillars: In one voyage
    Did Claribel her husband find at Tunis,
    And Ferdinand, her brother, found a wife
    Where he himself was lost, Prospero his dukedom
    In a poor isle, and all of us ourselves
    When no man was his own.[24]

[24]*When no man . . . own*] At a time when no one was in his senses.

ALON.　[to FER. and MIR.] Give me your hands:
　　　Let grief and sorrow still embrace his heart
　　　That doth not wish you joy!
GON.　　　　　　　　　　　　Be it so! Amen!

Re-enter ARIEL, with the MASTER and BOATSWAIN amazedly following.

　　　O, look, sir, look, sir! here is more of us:
　　　I prophesied, if a gallows were on land,
　　　This fellow could not drown. Now, blasphemy,
　　　That swear'st grace o'erboard, not an oath on shore?
　　　Hast thou no mouth by land? What is the news?
BOATS.　The best news is, that we have safely found
　　　Our king and company; the next, our ship—
　　　Which, but three glasses[25] since, we gave out split—
　　　Is tight and yare[26] and bravely rigg'd, as when
　　　We first put out to sea.
ARI.　[Aside to PROS.] Sir, all this service
　　　Have I done since I went.
PROS.　[Aside to ARI.] My tricksy spirit!
ALON.　These are not natural events; they strengthen
　　　From strange to stranger. Say, how came you hither?
BOATS.　If I did think, sir, I were well awake,
　　　I 'ld strive to tell you. We were dead of sleep,
　　　And—how we know not—all clapp'd under hatches;
　　　Where, but even now, with strange and several noises
　　　Of roaring, shrieking, howling, jingling chains
　　　And mo diversity of sounds, all horrible,
　　　We were awaked; straightway, at liberty;
　　　Where we, in all her trim, freshly beheld
　　　Our royal, good, and gallant ship; our master
　　　Capering to eye her:[27]—on a trice, so please you,
　　　Even in a dream, were we divided from them,
　　　And were brought moping hither.
ARI.　　　　　　　　[Aside to PROS.] Was 't well done?
PROS.　[Aside to ARI.] Bravely, my diligence. Thou shalt be free.
ALON.　This is as strange a maze as e'er men trod;
　　　And there is in this business more than nature
　　　Was ever conduct[28] of: some oracle
　　　Must rectify our knowledge.

[25]three glasses] "three hours" [see Act I, Sc. II, footnote 25]
[26]yare] fit, ready.
[27]Capering to eye her] Skipping about at sight of her.
[28]conduct] conductor, guide.

PROS.   Sir, my liege,
    Do not infest your mind with beating on
    The strangeness of this business; at pick'd leisure
    Which shall be shortly, single I 'll resolve you,
    Which to you shall seem probable, of every
    These happen'd accidents; till when, be cheerful,
    And think of each thing well. [*Aside to* ARI.] Come hither, spirit:
    Set Caliban and his companions free;
    Untie the spell. [*Exit* ARIEL.] How fares my gracious sir?
    There are yet missing of your company
    Some few odd lads that you remember not.

Re-enter ARIEL, *driving in* CALIBAN, STEPHANO, *and* TRINCULO, *in
their stolen apparel.*

STE.   Every man shift for all the rest, and let no man take care for him-
    self; for all is but fortune.—Coragio, bully-monster, coragio!
TRIN.   If these be true spies which I wear in my head, here 's a goodly
    sight.
CAL.   O Setebos, these be brave spirits indeed!
    How fine my master is! I am afraid
    He will chastise me.
SEB.   Ha, ha!
    What things are these, my lord Antonio?
    Will money buy 'em?
ANT.   Very like; one of them
    Is a plain fish, and, no doubt, marketable.
PROS.   Mark but the badges of these men, my lords,
    Then say if they be true. This mis-shapen knave,
    His mother was a witch; and one so strong
    That could control the moon, make flows and ebbs,
    And deal in her command, without her power.[29]
    These three have robb'd me; and this demi-devil—
    For he 's a bastard one—had plotted with them
    To take my life. Two of these fellows you
    Must know and own; this thing of darkness I
    Acknowledge mine.
CAL.   I shall be pinch'd to death.
ALON.   Is not this Stephano, my drunken butler?
SEB.   He is drunk now: where had he wine?

---

[29]*And deal . . . power*] And exercise the moon's own powers of control, while remaining
    outside the limits of her sovereignty.

ALON.   And Trinculo is reeling ripe:[30] where should they
    Find this grand liquor that hath gilded[31] 'em?—
    How camest thou in this pickle?
TRIN.   I have been in such a pickle, since I saw you last, that, I fear
    me, will never out of my bones: I shall not fear fly-blowing.[32]
SEB.   Why, how now, Stephano!
STE.   O, touch me not;—I am not Stephano, but a cramp.
PROS.   You 'ld be king o' the isle, sirrah?
STE.   I should have been a sore one, then.
ALON.   This is a strange thing as e'er I look'd on.

                              [*Pointing to* CALIBAN.

PROS.   He is as disproportion'd in his manners
    As in his shape. Go, sirrah, to my cell;
    Take with you your companions; as you look
    To have my pardon, trim it handsomely.
CAL.   Ay, that I will; and I 'll be wise hereafter,
    And seek for grace. What a thrice-double ass
    Was I, to take this drunkard for a god,
    And worship this dull fool!
PROS.   Go to; away!
ALON.   Hence, and bestow your luggage where you found it.
SEB.   Or stole it, rather.

                        [*Exeunt* CAL., STE., *and* TRIN.

PROS.   Sir, I invite your Highness and your train
    To my poor cell, where you shall take your rest
    For this one night; which, part of it, I 'll waste
    With such discourse as, I not doubt, shall make it
    Go quick away: the story of my life,
    And the particular accidents gone by
    Since I came to this isle: and in the morn
    I 'll bring you to your ship, and so to Naples,
    Where I have hope to see the nuptial
    Of these our dear-beloved solemnized;
    And thence retire me to my Milan, where
    Every third thought shall be my grave.
ALON.   I long
    To hear the story of your life, which must
    Take the ear strangely.

[30]*reeling ripe*] ripe for reeling (in drunkenness).
[31]*gilded*] a slang term for "made drunk."
[32]*shall not fear fly-blowing*] pickling was a preservative against "fly-blowing [*i.e.*, putre-
  faction by flies]."

PROS.   I 'll deliver all;
   And promise you calm seas, auspicious gales,
   And sail so expeditious, that shall catch
   Your royal fleet far off. [*Aside to* ARI.] My Ariel, chick,
   That is thy charge: then to the elements
   Be free, and fare thou well! Please you, draw near.   [*Exeunt.*

EPILOGUE

Spoken by Prospero.

Now my charms are all o'erthrown,
And what strength I have 's mine own,
Which is most faint: now, 't is true,
I must be here confined by you,
Or sent to Naples. Let me not,
Since I have my dukedom got,
And pardon'd the deceiver, dwell
In this bare island by your spell;
But release me from my bands
With the help of your good hands:[1]
Gentle breath of yours my sails
Must fill, or else my project fails,
Which was to please. Now I want
Spirits to enforce, art to enchant;
And my ending is despair,
Unless I be relieved by prayer,
Which pierces so, that it assaults
Mercy itself,[2] and frees all faults.
As you from crimes would pardon'd be,
Let your indulgence set me free.

[1] *With the help . . . hands*] With your applause; noise was held to dissolve a spell.
[2] *Mercy itself*] The Deity.

DOVER THRIFT EDITIONS

PLAYS

THE ORESTEIA TRILOGY: Agamemnon, the Libation-Bearers and the Furies, Aeschylus. (0-486-29242-8)

EVERYMAN, Anonymous. (0-486-28726-2)

THE BIRDS, Aristophanes. (0-486-40886-8)

LYSISTRATA, Aristophanes. (0-486-28225-2)

THE CHERRY ORCHARD, Anton Chekhov. (0-486-26682-6)

THE SEA GULL, Anton Chekhov. (0-486-40656-3)

MEDEA, Euripides. (0-486-27548-5)

FAUST, PART ONE, Johann Wolfgang von Goethe. (0-486-28046-2)

THE INSPECTOR GENERAL, Nikolai Gogol. (0-486-28500-6)

SHE STOOPS TO CONQUER, Oliver Goldsmith. (0-486-26867-5)

GHOSTS, Henrik Ibsen. (0-486-29852-3)

A DOLL'S HOUSE, Henrik Ibsen. (0-486-27062-9)

HEDDA GABLER, Henrik Ibsen. (0-486-26469-6)

DR. FAUSTUS, Christopher Marlowe. (0-486-28208-2)

TARTUFFE, Molière. (0-486-41117-6)

BEYOND THE HORIZON, Eugene O'Neill. (0-486-29085-9)

THE EMPEROR JONES, Eugene O'Neill. (0-486-29268-1)

CYRANO DE BERGERAC, Edmond Rostand. (0-486-41119-2)

MEASURE FOR MEASURE: Unabridged, William Shakespeare. (0-486-40889-2)

FOUR GREAT TRAGEDIES: Hamlet, Macbeth, Othello, and Romeo and Juliet, William Shakespeare. (0-486-44083-4)

THE COMEDY OF ERRORS, William Shakespeare. (0-486-42461-8)

HENRY V, William Shakespeare. (0-486-42887-7)

MUCH ADO ABOUT NOTHING, William Shakespeare. (0-486-28272-4)

FIVE GREAT COMEDIES: Much Ado About Nothing, Twelfth Night, A Midsummer Night's Dream, As You Like It and The Merry Wives of Windsor, William Shakespeare. (0-486-44086-9)

OTHELLO, William Shakespeare. (0-486-29097-2)

AS YOU LIKE IT, William Shakespeare. (0-486-40432-3)

ROMEO AND JULIET, William Shakespeare. (0-486-27557-4)

A MIDSUMMER NIGHT'S DREAM, William Shakespeare. (0-486-27067-X)

THE MERCHANT OF VENICE, William Shakespeare. (0-486-28492-1)

HAMLET, William Shakespeare. (0-486-27278-8)

RICHARD III, William Shakespeare. (0-486-28747-5)